Here Is Where We Meet

I admire and love John Berger's books. He writes about what is important, not just interesting. In contemporary English letters, he seems to me peerless; not since Lawrence has there been a writer who offers such attentiveness to the sensual world with responsiveness to the imperatives of conscience. Less of a poet than Lawrence, he is more intelligent and more citizenly, more noble. He is a wonderful artist and thinker.

Susan Sontag

It was he who showed me, before I knew anything, that literature is inimical to all hierarchies and that to separate fact and imagination, event and feeling, protagonist and narrator, is to stay on dry land and never put to sea.

John Berger on James Joyce

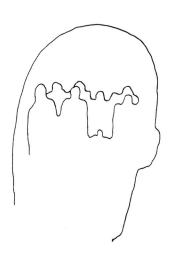

Here Is Where We Meet
John Berger: a season in London 2005

I can't tell you what art does and how it does it, but I know that art has often judged the judges, pleaded revenge to the innocent and shown to the future what the past has suffered, so that it has never been forgotten. I know too that the powerful fear art, whatever its form, when it does this, and that amongst the people such art sometimes runs like a rumour and a legend because it makes sense of what life's brutalities cannot, a sense that unites us, for it is inseparable from a justice at last. Art, when it functions like this, becomes a meeting-place of the invisible, the irreducible, the enduring, guts and honour.

John Berger

CULTURE | COLLABORATIONS | COMMITMENT

artevents

Curator & Catalogue Editor Gareth Evans
Producer Di Robson
Website & Publicity Design Emma Sangster
Catalogue Art Director John Christie
Catalogue Designer Jonathan Christie
PR Anna Arthur PR
Marketing artevents

Drawing on page 2 by Yves Berger

Readers and Writer Co-ordinators:
A Fortunate Man Gene Feder and Iona Heath
A Seventh Man Asu Aksoy, Kevin Robins
King Adrian Jackson
To the Wedding Jane Anderson

Season Advisory Group
Ruth Borthwick, Liz Calder, Chris Darke, Mike Dibb,
Geoff Dyer, Roger Elsgood, Jaune Evans, Dan Gretton,
Keith Griffiths, Chris Mitchell

With special thanks to
All at Bloomsbury Publishing, Cardboard Citizens,
John Christie, Alan Dein, Judith Dimant, Natasha Freedman,
Katherine Greenwood, London and Continental, Simon
McBurney, Anne Michaels, Jean Mohr, Michael Ondaatje,
Sukdev Sandhu, Verena Stackleberg, Jon Teeman

Thanks to our participating venues
Curzon Soho, German Gym, ICA, inIVA, London
Review Bookshop, Lyttelton Circle Foyer Gallery,
National Gallery, National Portrait Gallery, National
Theatre, Purdy Hicks Gallery, Queen Mary University,
Royal College of Physicians, Tate Britain

Published by artevents, 107 Mayola Road, London E5 0RG
for John Berger, Here Is Where We Meet:
A Season in London 2005.

ISBN 0-9549848-0-3

www.johnberger.org

John Berger: Here Is Where We Meet
was made possible with the financial and partnership support of:

Lannan Foundation is a family foundation dedicated to cultural freedom, diversity and creativity.
Understanding that globalization threatens all cultures and ecosystems, the foundation is
particularly interested in projects that encourage freedom of inquiry, imagination, and expression.

Partner Venues and Organisations:

As a legacy of this season the advisory committee and producers of
John Berger: Here Is Where We Meet are establishing a trust, the
Writing Now Foundation. This foundation will support emerging
writers and literature projects working in the "spirit" of John
Berger and his collaborators. To contribute to the foundation
and/or receive further information please call 020 8510 9786.

Contents

INTRODUCTION & LITERATURE 6

with Geoff Dyer, Anne Michaels, Michael Ondaatje, Timothy O'Grady

8   Biography
10 Preface *by Geoff Dyer*
12 Other Kinds of Dreams *by Sukhdev Sandhu*
16 Wanting Now *by John Berger*

FILM & TELEVISION 24

with Mike Dibb, Dai Vaughan, Chris Rawlence, Alain Tanner,
John Christie, Timothy Neat, Paul Carlin, Milena Trivier, Sally Potter

43 Filmography
45 War Against Terrorism or A Terrorist War? *By John Berger*
47 Orlando Letelier *by Anthony Barnett & John Berger*

VISUAL ART 48

with Jean Mohr, Iona Heath, Richard Hollis, John Christie,
Katya Berger Andreadakis, Maggi Hambling, Marc Trivier, Yves Berger

67 I Would Softly Tell My Love *by John Berger*

PERFORMANCE 72

with Anne Michaels, Simon McBurney and Complicite, Nella Bielski,
Despina Chronopoulos, Platform London, Cardboard Citizens

86 That Have Not Been Asked: Ten Dispatches about
      Endurance in Face of Walls *by John Berger*

90 Contributor Biographies
91 Bibliography

SEASON INFORMATION 92

INTRODUCTION
& LITERATURE
FILM &
TELEVISION
VISUAL ART
PERFORMANCE

Never again will a single story be told as though it were the only one. *John Berger*

One of the most internationally influential British writers of the last fifty years, John Berger has explored the relationship between the individual and society, culture and politics and the tension between experience and expression in a series of novels, bookworks, essays, plays, films, photographic collaborations and performances, unmatched in their diversity, ambition and reach. His television series and book *Ways of Seeing* (with Mike Dibb) revolutionised the way that Visual Art is perceived and read, while his engagement with European peasantry and migration in the fiction trilogy *Into Their Labours* and *A Seventh Man* stand as models of empathy and insight.

Central to his creative identity is the idea of collaboration, with places and communities as much as with other artists and thinkers. Democratic and open exchange is embedded into his approach, and among those with whom he has worked are some of the most imaginative in their fields, whether theatre directors like Complicite's Simon McBurney, artists Juan Munoz and John Christie, photographer Jean Mohr or film-makers Mike Dibb, Alain Tanner and Timothy Neat.

This publication accompanies the season *John Berger: Here Is Where We Meet*, taking place across London in April and May 2005; however, it also stands independently as a document of these collaborations. Like the season, it re-presents work that has previously proved difficult to experience, recontextualises well-known pieces and presents new and ongoing projects.

Due to the range of his creativity in all media, the totality of John's achievement is often overlooked. His internationalist perspective, and refusal to be contained within narrow definitions of what might constitute the life of a writer, has meant that few perhaps have encountered the full oeuvre. This unique overview of his explorations and encounters with others and the world offers a remarkable opportunity to consider what it means to be a committed artist in a rapidly changing and challenging period of our history.

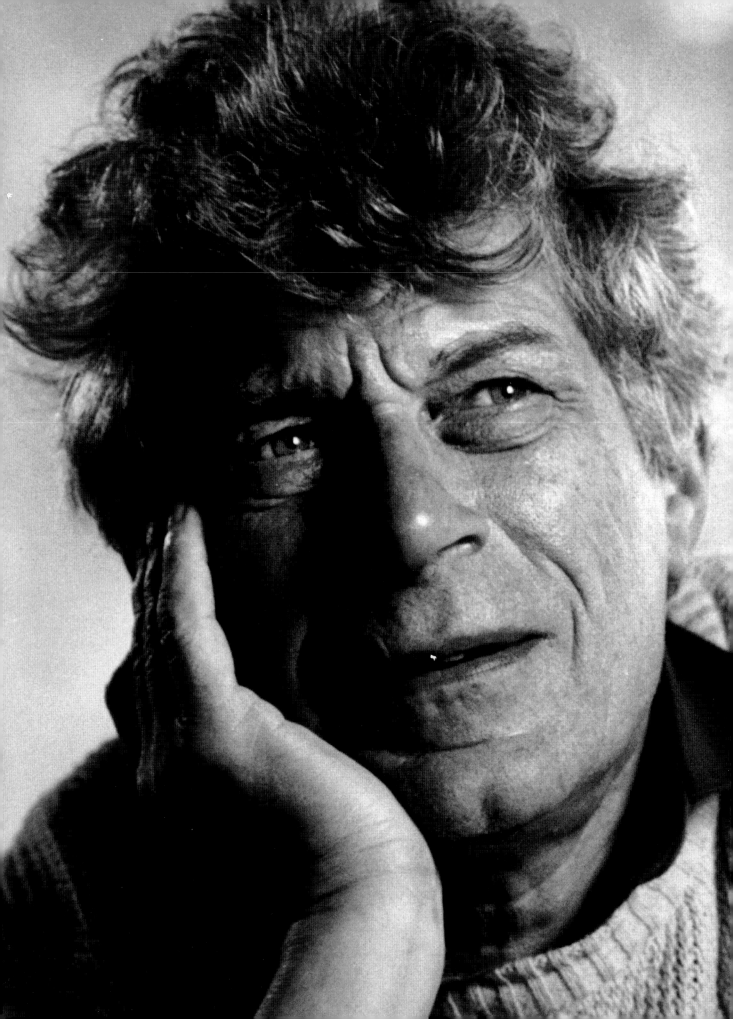

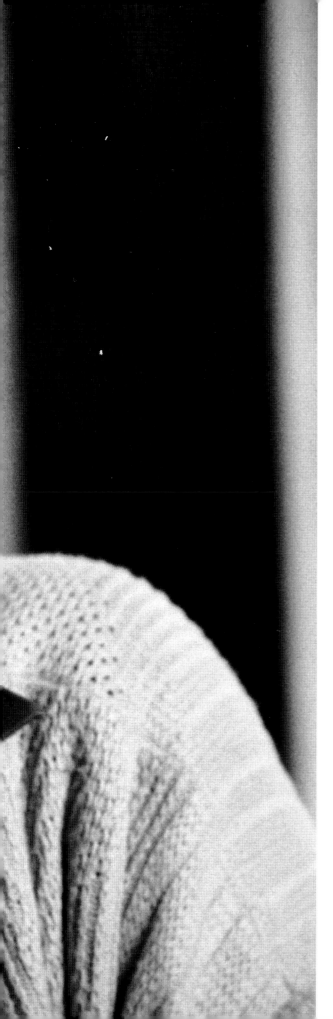

John Berger

John Berger is an internationally renowned story-teller, essayist, screen-writer and playwright. He was born in London in 1926 and, after studying at the Central and Chelsea Schools of Art, began to work as a painter and teacher of drawing, but soon turned to writing. In 1952 he began contributing to *The New Statesman*, and quickly became an influential commentator on Art. His books, innovative in form and far-reaching in their historical and political insight, include many publications on art and its relationship to society and power, not least the profoundly influential *Ways of Seeing*, which was also a television series, just one of the many documentary films and features he has made. In collaboration with the Swiss filmmaker Alain Tanner, John wrote the screenplays for *Jonah Who Will Be 25 in the Year 2000*, *Middle of the World* and *The Salamander*. He is, in addition, the author of three plays.

Beginning with his first novel *A Painter of Our Time* in 1958, John has also produced a significant body of fiction including *G.*, the 1972 winner of England's Booker Prize and the James Tait Black Memorial Prize, *To the Wedding* and *King*. His latest work, *Here Is Where We Meet*, is published to launch this season.

Central to his thinking is consideration of the relationship between text and image. With Swiss photographer Jean Mohr, he has made three books, *A Fortunate Man*, *A Seventh Man* and *Another Way of Telling*, that have engaged radically with this issue.

For the past thirty years John has lived in a small village in the French Alps. Exploring the traditions and changing way of life of the peasant community, he has written the remarkable fiction trilogy *Into Their Labours*, inspiration for the multi-award winning theatre piece *The Three Lives of Lucie Cabrol* by Complicite.

In 2002, he won the Lannan Foundation Lifetime Achievement Award.

JOHN CHRISTIE

Preface

by Geoff Dyer

I met John Berger for the first time in 1984. He was 'In Conversation' with Lisa Appignanesi at the ICA in London and afterwards he signed a copy of his new book, *And Our Faces, My Heart, Brief as Photos*, for me. A few days later he agreed to be interviewed by me for *Marxism Today*. (Ah, those were the days.)

Berger was my favourite writer in the world - and he was also the first writer I had actually met. There is a long and distinguished history of disappointment in such encounters. The writer you idolise turns out to have feet - and possibly legs, arms, even a brain - of clay; he turns out to be egotistical, vain, solipsistic, insufferable. The stakes were especially high in Berger's case because in order to live up to the standards of humanity, compassion and wisdom displayed in his books he would have to be an exceptional human being.

In our interview John was brilliant and forthcoming. Many writers are courteous and engaging in this situation but once the interview is over - i.e. once they have got the publicity their books need - they bring the encounter to a quick conclusion. When we had finished our interview John asked if I wanted to come to a pub for lunch and, of course, I agreed. In the pub he asked if I would like a Scotch Egg. I've always been a rather fussy eater and a Scotch egg is, by a considerable margin, the most disgusting form of food ever invented but because I was with John Berger I said, 'Yes, I'd love one.' I remember sitting there, eating this unbelievable thing and thinking to myself 'This is the greatest day of my life.' Many of the friends I'd been at college with were carving out careers for themselves (some even had mortgages!) while I was just living on the dole, smoking lots of grass, drifting in the name of some vague, infinitely postponable purpose. But on this day I had sprinted way ahead of all of my contemporaries because I was in a pub in London eating this disgusting Scotch Egg with John Berger who, as a man, turned out to be every bit as wonderful as his books. He was so kind, generous, attentive, interested. He even asked me to send him some of the stuff I'd written. When I did he wrote back immediately and encouragingly. He became a mentor in the vaguest and best way: he was

always encouraging. I was ready to be a disciple to his guru but since this relationship is actually a bore for both parties we gradually settled into being friends.

Irrespective of disparities of age or talent John longs for… No, let me re-phrase that, he simply has no patience for any relationships that are not relationships of equality. More than any of its perks or privileges John has enjoyed his success because it has allowed this predisposition to be absolutely confirmed. There is nothing humble about this: it's just that the potential of a hierarchical relationship with the world is exhausted in the instant that it is established.

On this day I had sprinted way ahead of all of my contemporaries because I was in a pub in London eating this disgusting Scotch Egg with John Berger, who turned out to be every bit as wonderful as his books.

(I am reminded of Barbara Ehrenreich's explanation, in *Nickel and Dimed*, of why, unlike many of her friends, she does not employ a cleaner: 'this is just not the kind of relationship I want to have with another human being.') It is for this reason - aside from his talent, the originality of his thought and so forth - that John has been such an enthusiastic and successful collaborator for so long. In *A Painter of Our Time* the narrator, Janos Lavin, writes, 'We can only learn from the success of our equals.' John has kept learning because he keeps putting himself in situations in which he can meet new and different equals.

Everyone who has encountered John in these or other situations will have observed his limitless capacity for giving. Partly this is the result of a natural, instinctive generosity. But I think he also realised that the artist's drive to achieve perfection in the work could only be maintained in collaboration with his continuing evolution as a man.

Other Kinds of Dreams
Why John Berger's writing matters

by Sukhdev Sandhu

Does writing have any meaning? The question lies heavily in my mind. Custom houses for words, incinerations of words, cemeteries for words are organised. So we will resign ourselves to live a life that is not ours. They force us to reorganise our alien memory as our own. Masked reality, history as told by the winners: perhaps writing is no more than an attempt to save, in times of infamy, the voices that will testify to the fact that we were here and this is how we were.

Eduardo Galeano, from *Days and Nights of Love and War* (1978)

"We were here and this is how we were." Few writers currently alive have attended more intently, more fiercely and more tenderly than John Berger to questions of who, what and how we - especially those of us in the Western world - were, are and may become. Spanning fiction, theatre, poetry, essays, radio, television and cinema, he has produced since the Second World War a huge and endlessly, roamingly diverse range of work. Sometimes it is self-created; just as often, it emerges through collaboration with other artists (even his most famous volume, *Ways of Seeing*, is described as 'A book made by John Berger, Sven Blomberg, Chris Fox, Michael Dibb, Richard Hollis'). A key characteristic is its ability to reconcile apparent antinomies, being at once obdurate and spring-heeledly agile, of direct appeal to the intellect and to the heart.

Probing excurses, travelogues through time as well as space, on topics such as the fortunes of Turkish guest workers in Germany, the disappearing world of European peasantry, the nature of memory in an age of accelerated cultural amnesia, the possibility of a revolutionary art in degraded times: to try to catalogue all the subject areas Berger has mined would be an arduous undertaking for researchers - and completely pointless. It would betray the spirit of his project, or rather projects, which are always on-going, future-orientated, more driven by a desire to keep abreast of and intervene in contemporary crises than to waste precious time dwelling over past triumphs. Chronologies of publication details and transmission dates can be left to biographers and postgraduate researchers. The best way to honour Berger is not to pore over every word he has written as if it came straight from the Talmud, or to memorise lengthy slabs of it in devotional parrotry, but to respond to the spirit of his work, one that to a large extent is encapsulated in the Italian philosopher Antonio Gramsci's edict about the necessity of a "pessimism of the intellect, an optimism of the will."

A large part of Berger's appeal today stems from his ambivalent relationship to the upper-middle-class English milieux he inhabited during his youth. He was educated at public school, served (extremely reluctantly) in the British Army from 1944-1946, and within a few years was writing for Orwell's Tribune before becoming art critic for the New Statesman. Schoolchildren, especially ambitious schoolboys, who grew up post-Austerity, were weaned, not just on Ken Tynan's scorched-earth disquisitions on contemporary drama in the Observer, but on Berger's equally revolutionary visual culture essays advocating critical realism and an anti-Imperial brand of Marxism. Thankfully, he was too earnest and not lazy enough, to fall in with the kitchen-sink 1956 And All That brigade, Amis and Osbourne and Braine, who within a few years had given themselves over to cardiganned carping, issuing morose mistake-of-the-nation jeremiads, and retreating into little-Englander mode.

Berger, like that other boss-class renegade Lindsay Anderson, resisted this creeping conservatism. He not only spoke about, but actually performed, important acts of rebellion. Awarded the Booker prize in 1972 for his novel *G.* he used the platform he had been given to denounce Booker McConnell's sugar-plantation holdings, arguing that, "the modern poverty of the Caribbean is the direct result of this and similar exploitation." Half his £5000 prize money he donated to the Black Panthers; the other half he used to fund research into contemporary migration. Such gestures, however in keeping with the revolutionary stirrings of the period, tend to be uncommon in the literary world. An equally welcome modern refusal came in 2003 when Hari Kunzru turned down the John Llewellyn Rhys Prize on the grounds that it was sponsored by the Mail on Sunday: "By accepting it I would have been giving legitimacy to a publication that has over many years shown itself to be extremely xenophobic, an absurdity for a novelist of mixed race, supposedly being honoured for a book about the stupidity of racial classifications and the seedy underside of Empire."

There is, to be sure, a valuable, if not always sufficiently valued, tradition of English dissent to which Berger partly belongs, one that extends from Cobbett and Hazlitt to DH Lawrence, Raymond Williams and even Ken Loach. These are artists who, for all their travels abroad, derive their catalysing energies from the soil and soul of England – or, in Williams's case, Wales. But the fact that Berger has lived outside the United Kingdom now for well over thirty years, in a small village in the French Alps, is not just a picturesque detail. It highlights the extent to which he has journeyed well beyond the parochialism of metropolitan intellectual life – its coercive triviality, its fetish of youth and of celebrity, its preference for burbling, self-referential opinionating rather than for more demanding and contemplative, provincial essays of the kind produced by relatively unfashionable writers such as Jeremy Seabrook, Ken Worpole and Byron Rodgers. Berger, like the theatre director Peter Brook, who was born a year earlier in 1925, opted out of this closed circle, and what he lost in terms of public profile he more than gained in breadth of vision, depth of studies and heightened moral conviction.

Perhaps it is this centrifugal motion in Berger's career – no, never a career: let's say life – that helps to explain *A Seventh Man* (1975), the extraordinarily prophetic and resonant prose poem-cum-photo essay on the topic of migrant workers that he assembled with his long-term collaborator Jean Mohr. It was written long before the contemporary interest in those people Jeremy Harding has called 'The Uninvited' – the refugees, asylum-seekers and immigrants who trek for days and weeks across mountains and seas, often in conditions not dissimilar from those faced by black slaves during the Middle Passage, in order to breach Fortress Europe and make new, better-paid lives for themselves.

A Seventh Man is no sociological report, no policy institute catalogue. Rather, it's a composite text whose own apparent fragmentation mirrors the fragmentation of its subjects, and comprises shards of oral testimony, strange anthropometric diagrams of the physical toll exerted by repetitive labour on migrants' bodies, passages that delve into gastarbeiter ontology, denunciations of the double-thinking political ideology that simultaneously summons these workers to Europe and then ostracises and ill-treats them. Mohr's photos, one of them showing a ripped shop receipt, another a blank space to illustrate the necessary invisibility of illegal settlers, depict the men's strength and loneliness; they do not merely illustrate Berger's writing, but, often presented in montage form, expand and build upon it. Throughout the book there is to be found that tense and animating wrestle between poetics and politics, that unceasing battle that courses through so many of Berger's writings: "Metaphor is needed. Metaphor is temporary. It does not replace theory."

Recently, I spent time with Able Miller, a Zimbabwean political refugee living in Glasgow. He told me: "Every time I get up I wonder: who am I? What's next? All my friends - it sounds funny, but I talk to dead people. Because when I go to sleep, all the people I talk to now, and all the people I dream about, are all people who are dead. And yet I still talk to them like they're alive." He added: "When you're somebody born with an identity, you have set goals and aims, and then suddenly you have no identity, and people don't even know who you are, you can't have goals. It's difficult even to describe an ambition. You just plod along from day to day." *A Seventh Man* is full of ghosts, men whose identities have been stretched and racked almost to breaking point. It does not try to discover their real personalities, or to trace individual pasts, but it does highlight, forcefully and hauntingly, the fact that they were not always the units of currency to which hostile politicians and tabloid-headline writers had reduced them. They were family men, intimacy-starved loners, epic pioneers. They were something more than zero.

Berger's achievement, like that of the Turkish workers, has been to cross and even to dissolve boundaries. His most important books, among them *A Fortunate Man* (1967) and *And Our Faces, My Heart, Brief as Photos* (1982), are vital

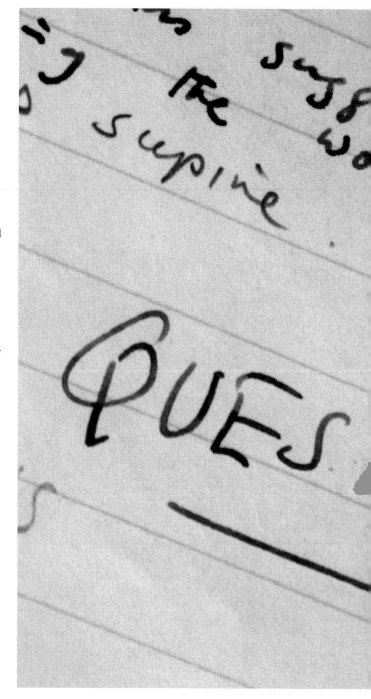

documents that prove the much-trumpeted death of the novel need not be a source of tragedy and that new forms of storytelling that combine travelogue, memoir, philosophical meditation, essay and photo journal can more eloquently describe the shifting modes of experience today. This traffic between genres prefigures that found in writers such as Sven Lindqvist, Ryszard Kapuscinski, WG Sebald and Eduardo Galeano, who have all in their different ways created a kind of rubble literature that has more in common with the sampling strategies of contemporary dance music than it does with the forms – the formulae even – of most contemporary fiction or historiography.

Berger should also be saluted for his contributions to the waning art of essay writing. The last forty years, broadly speaking the period in which various strands of continental philosophy have achieved pre-eminence in an increasingly specialised and intellectually less vagrant academy, have seen the rift between creative and critical writing grow deeper than ever before. Style and passion are regarded as belletristic. Most journals prefer clearly defined methodologies and forensic, personality-free prose styles. Berger, to a greater extent even than Susan Sontag, has maintained an individual voice that is fully informed about all manner of complex theories but is also comprehensible to the common reader. The large international audiences he has found for *Ways of Seeing* (1972), *About Looking* (1980) or *Another Way of Telling* (1982) attest to how successfully he has managed to re-orientate readers' gazes at aspects of the social world that they had not thought to peer at or even to think about. As much as, if not more than, the giants of poststructuralist or postmodern thought, it is Berger who has expanded the terrain of what are considered legitimate questions or fields of study in the humanities.

He is, in the best sense, a teacherly writer and performer. One is immediately struck by the sheer time and thought he devotes to a topic, his wonder and his acuity, his palpable excitement at the ideas that he appears to be working his way through, and by the way that what he's saying, while by no means provisional or likely to be repudiated any time soon, emerges so freshly-hatched as to appear extemporised. Berger comes alive in the act of telling stories. They too become real, visceral entities. What's more, the process of gleaning insights is almost as important as the insights themselves. So is the art of synthesising and relaying them in narrative form. To read him, or to see him on television (the latter being a regrettably rare experience these days), is to marvel at his gaze – full of a romantic suitor's intensity; his voice – almost trembling with conviction; his gait – never shambling, rather a prowling cat getting ready to leap.

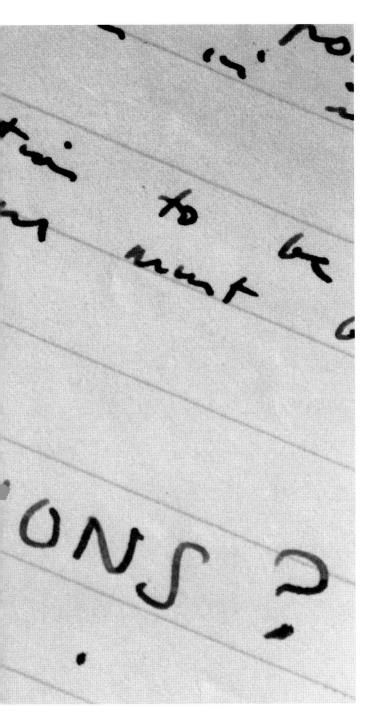

that convinces us that it need not always be that way. In spots of time – be they stumbled-upon or laboriously fashioned slithers of creativity, of human solidarity – we may grasp a guide rope to winch us from the sorrow of selfhood.

It would be easy, and tempting, to go on logging the innumerable reasons why John Berger's work has been, and continues to be, so inspirational to so many different audiences. A one-man hypertext, making links and connections between radically disparate times and places, he has managed to create a dialogue – no: seen the inextricability – of the poetic and the political, the local and the international, the past, present and future. That spirit also informs the books and moving images of many of the most important artists today, artists who I like to think of as working in the Berger idiom, artists who are formal or informal members of the Berger diaspora. That spirit is evident in *Etre et Avoir* (2002), the patient, tremulously beautiful chronicle of a year in a remote French primary school that was directed by an old Berger associate Nicholas Philibert. It is evident in *The Gleaners and I* (2000), Agnes Varda's stylistically innovative, playful but impassioned digicam essay about those outcasts and migrants who have to bend down and pick post-harvest produce or market-stall leftovers.

And in the example of Arundhati Roy. Ignoring the pleas of publishers and readers alike to bring out another book in the vein of her Booker Prize-winning novel *The God Of Small Things* (1998) she has dedicated herself, even at the cost of imprisonment, to campaigning against nuclear nationalism, dam-building and the abuse of adivasis: "There are other worlds," she writes in *The End of Imagination*, "other kinds of dreams. Dreams in which failure is feasible. Honourable. Sometimes even worth striving for. Worlds in which recognition is not the only barometer of brilliance or human worth. There are plenty of warriors that I know and love, people far more valuable than myself, who go to war each day, knowing in advance that they will fail." Who contributed the Introduction to that book? It was John Berger. His entire life's work has been dedicated to celebrating those other worlds, those other kinds of dreams.

Always, and this is fundamental to his ability to move across genres, he is passionate about the importance of imaginative translation: in *The Vertical Line* (1999), his collaboration with Complicite, he invited audience members to go down a disused underground station on the Strand in London the better to listen to his reflections on the Chauvet cave drawings; nearly 30 years earlier, he had illuminated Zola's *Germinal* by descending a Derbyshire coalmine for a 1972 Open University programme. Always in his work there is a felt knowledge that the world is a hard, abject, shitty place. And always in his work there is tenderness and beauty, a utopian, questing dimension

Wanting Now
A Thought for Trafalgar Square

by John Berger

The world has changed. Information is being communicated differently. Misinformation is developing its techniques. On a world scale emigration has become the principal means of survival. The national state of those who had suffered the worst genocide in history has become, militarily speaking, fascist. National states in general have been politically downsized and reduced to the role of vassals serving the new world economic order. The visionary political vocabulary of three centuries has been garbaged. In short, the economic and military global tyranny of today has been established.

At the same time new methods of resistance to this tyranny are being discovered. Rebels now have to be, not so much obedient as self-reliant. Within the resistance centralised authority has been replaced by spontaneous co-operation. Long-term programmes have been replaced by urgent alliances over specific issues. Civil society is learning and beginning to practice the guerilla tactics of political opposition.

Today the desire for justice is multitudinous.

That is to say that struggles against injustice, struggles for survival, for self-respect, for human rights, should never be considered merely in terms of their immediate demands, their organisations, or their historical consequences. They cannot be reduced to "movements". A movement describes a mass of people collectively moving towards a definite goal, which they either achieve or fail to achieve. Yet such a description ignores, or does not take into account, the countless personal choices, encounters, illuminations, sacrifices, new desires, griefs and, finally, memories, which the movement brought about, but which are, in the strict sense, incidental to that movement. The promise of a movement is its future victory; whereas the promises of the incidental moments are instantaneous. Such moments include, life-enhancingly or tragically, experiences of freedom in action. (Freedom without actions does not exist.) Such moments - as no historical "outcome" can ever be - are transcendental, are what Spinoza would have termed eternal, and they are as multitudinous as the stars in an expanding universe.

A growing awareness throughout the world of this truth is changing the politics of protest. The infinite is beside the poor.

Not all desires lead to freedom, but freedom is the experience of a desire being acknowledged, chosen and pursued. Desire never concerns the mere possession of something but the changing of something. Desire is a wanting. A wanting now. Freedom does not constitute the fulfilment of that wanting, but the acknowledgement of its supremacy.

If this is true, it follows that artists, no less than those involved in civic and political struggles, can sometimes join without, as it were, a second thought, that wanting now - and in so doing merge for a moment into a freedom which is eternal, and which bears no relation at all to the crap being spoken today by the new tyrants.

Language Is the House…

by Anne Michaels

Language is the house with lamplight in its windows,
visible across fields. Approaching, you can hear
music; closer, smell
soup, bay leaves, bread – a meal for anyone
who has only his tongue left.
It's a country; home; family:
abandoned; burned down; whole lines dead, unmarried.
For those who can't read their way in the streets,
or in the gestures and faces of strangers,
language is the house to run to;
in wild nights, chased by dogs and other sounds,
when you've been lost a long time,
when you have no other place.

There are nights in the forest of words
when I panic, every step into thicker darkness,
the only way out to write myself into a clearing,
which is silence.
Nights in the forest of words
when I'm afraid we won't hear each other
over clattering branches, over
both our voices calling.

In winter, in the hour
when the sun runs liquid then freezes,
caught in the mantilla of empty trees;
when my heart listens
through the cold stethoscope of fear,
your voice in my head reminds me
what the light teaches.
Slowly you translate fear into love,
the way the moon's blood is the sea.

From *What the Light Teaches*
from the collection *Miner's Pond*

It's no metaphor to feel the influence of the dead in the world, just as it's no metaphor to hear the radiocarbon chronometer, the Geiger counter amplifying the faint breathing of rock, fifty thousand years old. (Like the faint thump from behind the womb wall.) It is no metaphor to witness the astonishing fidelity of minerals magnetised, even after hundreds of millions of years, pointing to the magnetic pole, minerals that have never forgotten magma whose cooling off has left them forever desirous. We long for place; but place itself longs. Human memory is encoded in air currents and river sediment. Eskers of ash wait to be scooped up, lives reconstituted.

How many centuries before the spirit forgets the body? How long will we feel our phantom skin buckling over rockface, our pulse in magnetic lines of force? How many years pass before the difference between murder and death erodes?

   Grief requires time. If a chip of stone radiates its self, its breath, so long, how stubborn might be the soul. If sound waves carry on to infinity, where are their screams now? I imagine them somewhere in the galaxy, moving forever toward the psalms.

From *Fugitive Pieces*

On a photograph by Robert Capa

by Geoff Dyer

Works of art urge us to respond in kind and so, looking at a photograph by Robert Capa, my reaction expresses itself as a vow: I will never love another photograph more.

The caption on the back of the postcard on which I first saw it read: 'Italian soldier after end of fighting, Sicily 1943.' The allies invaded Italy in July of that year; Palermo, the capital, was captured on 22 July, and by 17 August the whole of Sicily was in Allied hands. Victory in Europe was still almost two years distant but Robert Capa's photo is like a premonition of - and coda to - the end of the war in Europe.

When I next saw the picture, in a book of Capa's work, it had a different caption. This time it read: 'Near Nicosia, Sicily July 28, 1943. An Italian soldier straggling behind a column of his captured comrades as they march off to a POW camp'. This is much more specific - but which of the two most accurately expresses the truth of the image (as opposed to the circumstances in which it was made)?

At first it seems that the entire meaning of the picture changes according to the caption but then one realises that whatever the circumstances surrounding the picture frame, Capa has deliberately isolated this young couple (making both captions misleading since neither mentions the woman). As Steinbeck remarked, Capa's 'pictures are not accidents.' Following Capa's example, I too prefer to 'crop' the narrative, to concentrate on the story contained by the image, to transcribe the caption inscribed within it.

Capa's picture recalls and complements another: André Kertész's photograph of 'A Red Hussar Leaving, June 1919, Budapest'. In the midst of the commotion of departure, a man and a woman look at each other for what may turn out to be the last time. In *Another Way of Telling*, John Berger writes of how the look that passes between them is an attempt to store the memory of this moment against everything that may happen in the future. Capa's photograph shows the moment when all the unvoiced hopes in that photograph - in that look - come true. And not just the hopes of Kertész's couple, but the hopes of all lovers separated by war.

The hot Mediterranean landscape. Dust on the bicycle tyres. The sun on her tanned arms. Their shadows mingling.

The flutter of butterflies above the tangled hedgerow. The crumbling wall at the field's edge is the result not of the sudden obliteration of bombs, but of the slow attrition of the seasons. It is possible to grow old in this landscape. The photograph would be diminished without the bicycle; it would be ruined without her long hair. Her hair says: this is how she was when he left, she has not changed, she has remained true to him.

Noticing these things fills me with longing. I want to be that soldier. Since that is impossible I resolve to go on a cycling holiday in Sicily. I want, also, to know their story. When did they meet? Have they made love? How long have they been walking? Where are they heading? How long is the journey? The photograph itself urges us to ask questions like this, but, if we look - and listen - hard it will provide the answers. Listen...

They do not care how long the walk ahead of them is; the greater the distance, the longer they can be together like this. She will ask about the things that have happened to him; he will be hesitant at first, but there is no hurry. She begins to remember his silence, the way it was implied by his handwriting, by the letters he sent. Eventually, he will tell her of the friends he has lost, the terrible things he has seen. He is impatient for news of friends and relatives, back in their village or town.

She will tell about her brother, who was also in the army and who was wounded, about his parents, about the funny thing that happened to the school teacher and the butcher's dog. They will walk along, their shoulders bumping, noticing everything about each other again, each a little apprehensive of disappointing the other in some small way. At some stage, perhaps when they are resting by the roadside or perhaps when they lie down to sleep under the star-clogged sky, she will turn to him and say, 'Am I still as pretty as when you left?' Knowing what his answer will be, feeling the roughness of his hand as he pushes the hair behind her ear, watching his mouth as he says, 'More. Much more.'

And the defeat of Italy, the end of the war? Maybe they will talk of that too, but not now, not now...

The Great Tree

by Michael Ondaatje

'Zou Fulei died like a dragon breaking down a wall …

this line composed and ribboned
in cursive script
by his friend the poet Yang Weizhem

whose father built a library
surrounded by hundreds of plum trees

It was Zou Fulei, almost unknown,
who made the best plum flower painting
of any period

One branch lifted into the wind

and his friend's vertical line of character

their tones of ink
– wet to opaque
dark to pale

each sweep and gesture
trained and various
echoing the other's art

In the high plum-surrounded library
where Yang Weizhem studied as a boy

a moveable staircase was pulled away
to ensure his solitary concentration

His great work
'untrammelled' 'eccentric' 'unorthodox'
'no taint of the superficial'
        'no flamboyant movement'

using at times the lifted tails
of archaic script,

sharing with Zou Fulei
his leaps and darknesses

                *

'So I have always held you in my heart …

The great 14th-century poet calligrapher
mourns the death of his friend

Language attacks the paper from the air

There is only a path of blossoms

no flamboyant movement

A night of smoky ink in 1361
a night without a staircase

From the collection *Handwriting*

Here Is Where We Meet

by John Berger

Greengages

We looked for greengages every year during the month of August. Frequently they disappointed. Either they were unripe, fibrous, almost dry, or else they were over-soft and mushy. Many were not worth biting into, for one could feel with one's finger that they did not have the right temperature: a temperature unfindable in Celsius or Fahrenheit: the temperature of a particular coolness surrounded by sunshine. The temperature of a small boy's fist.

The boy is somewhere between eight and ten-and-a-half years old, the age of independence, before the press of adolescence. The boy holds the greengage in his hand, brings it to his mouth, bites, and the fruit darts its tongue against the back of his throat so that he swallows its promise.

A promise of what? Of something that has not yet been named and he will soon name. He tastes a sweetness which no longer has anything to do with sugar, but with a limb that goes on and on, and seems to have no end. The limb belongs to a body which he can only see with his eyes shut. The body has three more limbs and a neck and ankles and is like his own; except that it is inside out. Through the limb without end flows a sap – he can taste it between his teeth – the sap of a nameless pale wood, which he calls girl-tree.

It was enough that one greengage in a hundred reminded us of that.

Cherries

In cherries, there was the flavour of fermentation as in no other fruit. Picked straight from the trees, they tasted of enzymes laced with the sun and this taste was complementary with the special shiny polish of their skins.

Eat cherries - even one hour after they have been picked - and their taste blends with that of their own rottenness. In the gold or red of their colour there is always a hint of brown: the colour into which they will soften and disintegrate.

The cherry refreshes, not on account of its purity - as does the apple - but by slightly, almost imperceptibly, tickling the tongue with the effervescence of its fermenting.

Because of the small size of the cherry and the lightness of its flesh and the insubstantiality of its skin, the cherry stone was always incongruous. The eating of the cherry never quite prepared you for its stone. When you spat it out, it seemed to have little connection with the flesh that surrounded it. It felt more like a precipitate of your own body, a precipitate mysteriously produced by the act of eating cherries. After each cherry you spat out a cherry tooth.

Lips, as distinct from the rest of the face, have the same gloss as cherries do and the same malleability. Both their skins are like the skin of a liquid. A question of their capillary surfaces. Make a test to see whether our memory is correct or whether the dead exaggerate. Put a cherry in your mouth, don't bite it yet, now for a split second remark how the density, the softness and the resilience of the fruit match perfectly the nature of your lips which hold it.

From 'Some Fruit as Remembered by the Dead' in *Here Is Where We Meet*

Reading John Berger

by Timothy O'Grady

I read *G.* when I was twenty-two on a deserted island off the coast of Donegal in Ireland. Amid the political convulsions, the aeronautical displays and the amorous encounters in this book so unlike any other I had ever read I found its author intermittently appearing on the page amidst his creations telling us his readers what he was seeing and thinking and dreaming as he struggled to bring to life the scenes we had just been reading or were about to read. Here was a picture of a man carrying a large idea toward which he was striving to be true, showing us his own doubt and tentativeness while page after page he opened doors to new things that the novel could do. I had been until then a kind of acolyte in a "death of the novel" cult, its principal texts written by academics disguised as novelists who declared that James Joyce had blasted away the foundations of the form, William Burroughs had administered the coup de grace, and that all that remained was to play around in its ashes in sustained parody of the act of writing itself. These novelists too occasionally appeared in their books, but only to say how futile it all was. John Berger was practicing the art of the possible.

Books, perhaps even more than the stories offered by life, can give a person the appetite to write, and then show him the way. I read *G.* with a growing fascination and a rising energy that carried me beyond its pages and into my own hopes of what I might do.

I kept looking for him after that. I read *A Seventh Man, A Painter of Our Time, A Fortunate Man.* He was there again in the fore- or background of each of these books, and he was vividly and nervously present in *Pig Earth,* learning along with his readers of the Alpine peasant life in which he was living and of which he had begun to write as he looked microscopically at the killing of a pig or the mating of goats. By the time he wrote *Once in Europa* he was on more easeful collaborative terms with his subjects in the village and with *Lilac and Flag* he was confident enough to disappear into the voice of an old woman. It was beautifully and tragically rendered, but I missed him. These three books formed *Into Their Labours,* a record of the leakage of village into metropolis, of meaning into incoherence. This, in my opinion, is one of the great works in English of the past half-century – though you would be hard pressed to know this from the words expended on it in the literary press or even to find it in a bookstore.

I went on to read *To the Wedding, Photocopies, And Our Faces, My Heart, Brief as Photos, King* and numerous other journalistic, political, critical, theatrical and poetical works. I've read far more books by him than by any other writer, dead or alive.

Somewhere along the way I finally began after a long wait to write sentences of my own in which I could believe. He was there as standard, guide, potential reader or spectral ventriloquist as I wrote them. When I was asked to write a text to accompany photographs taken in Ireland by Steve Pyke I would have had no idea how to proceed had I not had his books on which to lean. I would not have written of rural life as I did had I not read *Pig Earth,* of migration were it not for *A Seventh Man,* nor have found a way to put photographs and texts together had I not studied his collaborations with Jean Mohr. The book became a novel called *I Could Read the Sky* and it wouldn't have been a novel at all had I not seen his arranging of photographs, unaccompanied by words, into a work of fiction in *Another Way of Telling.* He fathered the book along each step of its gestation, execution and even its physical production. Another writer might have thought it touched the borders of plagiarism. He graced it with a preface.

What does he do? The great Irish fiddle player Martin Hayes told me that his music gained in power when he ceased to decorate and played only the notes essential to the tune. John's sentences are like that. He has both the humility and the confidence not to stand in their way and in consequence they have the simple purity of object, thought, feeling in themselves, unadorned. His frame is wider in both form and content than any other writer I know and each work has, as Michael Ondaatje has said, "broken the vessel they were written within in some way". He has pondered form, objects, the expression of others and the real world around us with its traumas and glories and brought forth works that carry the feeling of revelation. I was fortunate to have found him on the island in Donegal. I wish the world knew him better.

I Could Read the Sky

When I lie in bed in the evening I think ever and ever of money and of Kate Creevy. What is the distance between me and her? I see her walking ahead of me in the town. She's a basket on her arm and she's wearing a hat. A hat! It wasn't Sunday. She's a long stride but it's very light. I can see the line of her leg under her skirt. Sometimes her foot turns on a stone in the path and she has to right herself. I'd be there to catch her if she fell. She has gloves on a colour grey like a pigeon's breast. Her hair pinned up, the sweep of it over her ear, the long lines of her neck. The heartbeat is booming my head. I take the tin box out from under the bed. £1 2s. 6d. I lost a pound on Sunday in the gambling pit. I begin to count. I can put four shillings in the box each week. Times four. Sixteen shillings. Times twelve. £9 12s. for the year. I give names to the numbers as I think of them. Bonham. Blade. Set of delft. Horse. Black frieze coat to keep her warm. Whitewash. Barrel of porter. Bed. What is the distance between me and her?

What I could do.

I could mend nets. Thatch a roof. Build Stairs. Make a basket from reeds. Splint the leg of a cow. Cut turf. Build a wall. Go three rounds with Joe in the ring Da put up in the barn. I could dance sets. Read the sky. Make a barrel for mackerel.

Mend roads. Make a boat. Stuff a saddle. Put a wheel on a cart. Strike a deal. Make a field. Work the swarth turner, the float and the thresher. I could read the sea. Shoot straight. Make a shoe. Shear sheep. Remember poems. Set potatoes. Plough and harrow. Read the wind. Tend bees. Bind wyndes. Make a coffin. Take a drink. I could frighten you with stories. I knew the song to sing to a cow when milking. I could play twenty seven tunes on my accordion.

What I couldn't do.

Eat a meal lacking potatoes. Trust banks. Wear a watch. Ask a woman to go for a walk. Work with drains or with objects smaller than a nail. Drive a motor car. Eat tomatoes. Remember the routes of buses. Wear a collar in comfort. Win at cards. Acknowledge the Queen. Abide loud voices. Perform the manners of greeting and leaving. Save money. Take pleasure in work carried out in a factory. Drink coffee. Look into a wound. Follow cricket. Understand the speech of a man from west Kerry. Wear shoes or boots made from rubber. Best P.J. in an argument. Speak with men wearing collars. Stay afloat in water. Understand their jokes. Face the dentist. Kill a Sunday. Stop remembering.

From *I Could Read the Sky* by Timothy O'Grady

INTRODUCTION
& LITERATURE

FILM &
TELEVISION

VISUAL ART

PERFORMANCE

At the heart of John Berger's oeuvre lies a prolific body of work (features, series and documentaries) in film and television, which has never been gathered previously anywhere in the world. This is in some ways surprising, given that the medium has spawned perhaps his most well-known and influential single work (*Ways of Seeing*) and one of the most important films of the 1970s (*Jonah Who Will be 25 in the Year 2000*). However, such a retrospective is central to any understanding of how John has sought constantly to innovate the medium in which he finds himself, testing its limits for sustained aesthetic and political investigation. The programmes utterly resist the reduction of their participants to monotoned consumers of lifestyle product, and rather, they celebrate the power of ideas and the processes of thought, as well as demonstrating empathy in a way that is almost completely absent from today's broadcast schedules.

It is also the medium in which one of his longest-standing and most important collaborators operates. Documentary film-maker Mike Dibb created *Ways of Seeing* with John, and they have gone on to create some of their most significant work as part of this pairing, along with the singular skills of Chris Rawlence and acclaimed documentary editor Dai Vaughan. Add in *Another Way of Telling*, his series on photography with John Christie (and inspired by the book of the same name), and there is more evidence of how his projects can mutate across media with fresh and distinctive results.

But John's moving-image work has also extended beyond television onto the cinema screen in two significant partnerships; firstly with the Swiss film-maker Alain Tanner. Together they made three formally innovative, politically and narratively radical features in the 1970s that have sadly been all-too little seen since their making. Similarly, John's collaboration with writer, historian and film-maker Timothy Neat in the fiercely independent British feature *Play Me Something* explored both filmic narrative and the nature of storytelling in general at a time when the mainstream national film culture into which it emerged was – and remains – severely limited in its language and vision.

Alongside these major initiatives, John has remained constantly active in the medium, contributing scripts, ideas and his own involvement to a host of film-makers, from Sally Potter (and her important new feature *Yes*) to award-winning documentary maker Paul Carlin and emergent talent Milena Trivier. This makes perfect sense; with word and image so naturally a part of the filmic landscape, the medium suits his keen appreciation of the fecund conversations they can have.

On Documentary
Re-Seeing Ways of Seeing

by Mike Dibb

I still have all the versions of the four scripts that made up the
series we called *Ways of Seeing*. Reading them now, after 30
years, I'm struck by how much John wrote and re-wrote
(mostly in a back room of his parents' flat in Hallam St, just
behind Broadcasting House) and how much we changed right
up to the moment of filming and then modified during the
editing, with David Gladwell, after John returned to his home
in Geneva. For instance, the first film originally began with
John telling a short fable. But it felt flat, as did a potentially
striking sequence which happened a little later, in which John
with a sharp knife cut out a head from Botticelli's *Venus and*

Mars. I thought it would be interesting to try losing the story
and bring the Botticelli sequence to the head of the film,
juxtaposing it with a commentary for which it hadn't been
intended. Immediately that 'act of vandalism' gave the series
the dramatic send-off we needed.

   Because we were able to edit across a period of months, we
could film additional material when first ideas didn't work or
better ones occurred. (Which is, of course, why John's hair
suddenly changed halfway through Programme One!). And
sometimes we were lucky. We spent one day filming at a
primary school in South London. Having played a number of
games with pictures and words, none of which really worked,
we showed the children a reproduction of Caravaggio's
Supper at Emmaus. Miraculously something began to happen
and their spontaneous and perceptive comments created one

"Dear Mike, Here's script no.2. Please remember all I said about it on the phone. Criticise, improvise, change, improve, cancel out, as much as you want or see how to. Or even we can begin again. All I would stand by is the essential idea…"

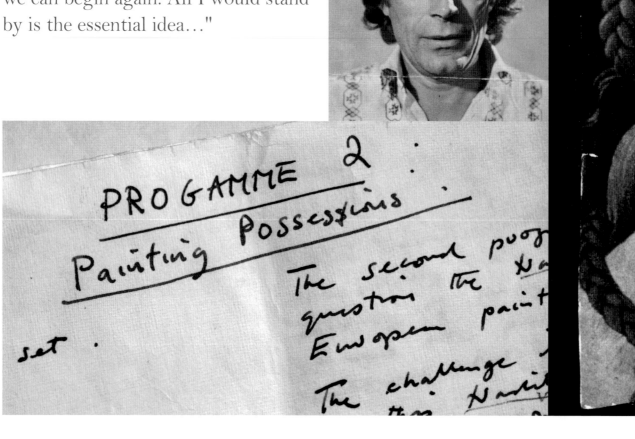

of the first film's most memorable sequences.

What I'm trying to say is that *Ways of Seeing* wasn't conceived to illustrate a thesis. It was always a journey of discovery. It began (as yet untitled) when Stephen Hearst, the BBC's Head of Music and Arts, asked John whether he would like to develop a short series about painting on themes of his choice. I was always going to be a part of it - I'd already met John in 1969 and, as a teenager, been greatly influenced by his writing since reading his art column in the New Statesman back in the 1950's - but, as a lowly assistant arts producer, I didn't think I'd be allowed to direct more than an episode or two. However, as John and I started to research the ideas, it became clear to everyone that the collaboration was working and I was given the responsibility of producing and directing the whole thing. John's first crucial decision, from which everything else in the series flowed, was to use as our point of departure some of the ideas in Walter Benjamin's essay *The Work of Art in the Age of Mechanical Reproduction*, which had

recently appeared in English. How could we translate Benjamin's brilliant but very dense text into an accessible television film, which would be both provocative and playful?

Although *Ways of Seeing* may appear to be a succession of statements, these statements are really questions. When John speaks in conversation his sentences often end with an interrogative. "No?" he says , inviting a response, not automatic assent. This is also true of his letters: "Dear Mike, Here's script no.2. Please remember all I said about it on the phone. Criticise, improvise, change, improve, cancel out, as much as you want or see how to. Or even we can begin again. All I would stand by is the essential idea…." This exemplary approach to collaboration characterised how we worked on *Ways of Seeing*, and on subsequent films together. Which does not mean that the process was always easy and free of tension (with John it's never like that), but the arguments, when they arose, were always open and ultimately resolved, not through theory, but by trying out an idea in practise to see if it worked.

And I often remember us laughing.

We were granted remarkable freedom (almost unthinkable in today's over-controlled TV climate) - by the executive producer John Drummond (now Sir John) - to discover, during the process of making the series, in what direction the films should evolve. This freedom also derived from the trust that was then conventionally given by Channel Controllers to individual programme departments and from the departments, in turn, to the producers who worked in them. I'm sure it also helped that the budget was small and so there was nothing much financially at stake.

Even after we began filming, we had no idea what the fourth film should be. For a while its proposed subject was the 'market'. We also played with ideas for deconstructing the meaning of 'national heritage'. Then one Sunday evening John phoned me from Richmond. He'd been to have lunch with Huw Wheldon (mastermind of the BBC's first arts magazine *Monitor*, for which John had earlier made several

films). On the way there John had looked at the ads on the escalators and walls of the underground. He'd noticed, not only how advertisers occasionally used the images and status of European art to sell their products, but also to what extent the iconography of these painted images was being co-opted and re-deployed by advertising, with colour photography assuming the function that oil paint once had. From that phone call the last and possibly most original film in the series was born.

There are two questions I'm often asked. Why the blue screen and why that shirt? The answers are connected. It was in the early days of CSO (colour separation overlay). Our original idea was that, because John would travel nowhere (in deliberate contrast to Kenneth Clarke) the paintings would have to 'travel' to him, so he should be filmed in a TV studio in front of a blue screen, with images electronically layered in behind. I soon realised it would be impossible to make the programmes this way, because video tape editing was then too cumbersome and crude, and I needed the flexibility of film.

In the half hour which was all his schedule allowed,
John came up with the idea that the text should be
re-written from the viewpoint of the animals themselves.
It was a suggestion which transformed the film.

But the idea of the blue screen stayed. I considered filming on one of the Ealing film stages, but it was too expensive. So we hired very cheaply a nearby electrical goods warehouse and brought our mobile blue screen there. This meant that John, unable to wear his normal blue shirt, had to go off and buy something without any blue in it. He arrived with what has provoked so much comment over the years, a pair of identical cream and red 'chain-mail' shirts, circa 1971. We didn't give them a second thought then, and now they're iconic!

Another thing that has always amused me is that out there in the darkness, on either side of John in his shirt delivering words of wisdom in front of a celestial screen, was *Ways of Seeing's* first silent audience, a packed house of fridges, TV sets and cookers! Little did we imagine what influence this modest little series would have and how many arguments it would engender. In the subsequent book, on which five of us worked, we tried to carry on in the same spirit, reversing the conventions of books about art. Among other things we used a heavy black type-face, small black and white reproductions embedded within the text rather than separated out into full-page plates, and tried to make it the cheapest art book then available, just 60p for the first edition.

"Consider what I say, but be sceptical..." said John at the end of the first film. "To be continued…" we wrote at the end of the book. Maybe that's why both are still alive.

On Editing

by Dai Vaughan

It was at the 1958 Easter march to Aldermaston that I first met John Berger. He zoomed off on his motorcycle to bring beer and sandwiches for a group of us who were taking a breather at the roadside. What is surprising in retrospect is to realise that he was already, for us, on the strength of a few years as *New Statesman* art critic and prehaps an appearance or two on Huw Wheldon's *Monitor*, a major figure in British cultural life. When *Permanent Red* appeared, in 1960, it was

not as an unheralded phenomenon but as the book everybody had been waiting for.

Sometimes, to a film editor, a locale we have assembled from visual and aural images can remain as vivid in our memory as one we have visited. This is true for me of the village represented in *Pig Earth* (1979), a BBC film directed by Mike Dibb in close association with John and based upon his book of that name. Direct address to the camera alternates with still photographs by Jean Mohr – black-and-white for human interaction, colour for architectural detail and countryside, plus some grainy super-8 home movie footage – to create an ambience remote as an analysis yet at the same time intimate as a dream. My main recollection of cutting this film, with Howard Sharp, is that no-one ever seemed to complain at how long we wanted to hold a shot.

John's own sensitivity to editing can best be illustrated by reference to *Parting Shots from Animals* (1980), an elaboration of ideas set out in his essay 'Why Zoos Disappoint'. At a crucial stage in the process, when we had assembled all the sequences with linking passages from the essay, John came to view what we had done. We ourselves were far from happy with it, but could not see the way forward. In the half hour which was all his schedule allowed, John came up with the idea that the text should be re-written from the viewpoint of the animals themselves and that this should be reinforced by the crew being shown from time to time wearing animal masks. It was a suggestion which transformed the film.

Something which has always impressed me, especially in later work such as the *About Time* series, where his involvement has been less direct, has been John's willingness to permit his own ideas, hard-won and assiduously crafted as they clearly are in his writings, to be developed in other media by other groups of people. There is an extraordinary lack of possessiveness here. Recent developments in video technology make it possible for a film to be directed, shot, recorded and edited by one person alone. Good films will be made this way. But the eradication of a practice of creative collaboration is surely a tremendous loss.

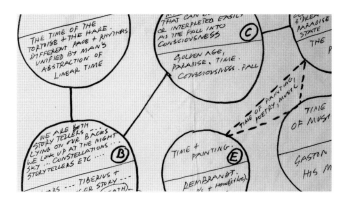

About Time

by Chris Rawlence

We were rehearsing in what had once been the Green Room of the London School of Economics theatre. For several years, five evenings a week, we would hammer out the group's politics, shape new plays, and develop the Red Ladder Theatre Company as an effective and popular theatre for the Trade Union Movement.

It was on one of those evenings in 1971 that John Berger came into the room. He was with Mike Dibb and, together, they were still working on *Ways of Seeing*. Mike had a hunch that he could adapt our visual style to sequences in the series.

So we talked. By day, I ran History of Art at the Slade and John's writing had been hugely helpful to my teaching. Particularly, his essay *The Moment of Cubism* had helped me reconcile my developing politics with my Courtauld Institute training as an art historian.

Nothing immediate came from that first LSE meeting. Some of our group were suspicious of involvement with television, viewing it as a corrupting bourgeois tool. In the event, John and Mike found a defter solution for the Gainsborough – a 'Trespassers will be Prosecuted' sign overlaid on the proud landowner's wheat fields in the background.

Our next encounter occurred in 1973 just before publication of John's book *A Seventh Man*. Mike and John were planning a BBC film of the book and, once again, it occurred to them that Red Ladder could provide a stylised visual dissection of the economics and politics that underlay a Turkish migrant worker's life in Germany. There was a more positive group reaction this time but this time the collaboration foundered when the BBC decided against producing the programme.

More years passed. When I left Red Ladder in 1979, Mike suggested that I might like to research a programme about animals, based on three essays John had written for New Society. I leapt at the chance.

Parting Shots from Animals (1980) looked at pets, Esso tigers, draught horses, zoos… and was not so much about animals as what we can understand about ourselves through our relationship to animals. In a way typical of John – with some help from Brecht - we turned the tables. Through an act of conscious projection we imagined what animals might think about us. It was again, but in a different way, about challenging the ways we see.

Parting Shots… paved the way for *About Time* (1984), a six part series that Mike and I made with John – as series consultant - for Channel 4. The premise was that, in the West, linear measured time – GMT and industrial time – dominated most other manifestations and experiences of time and made life poorer as a consequence. There was a programme of stories told by John, 'stories…' as he put it in the book that accompanied the series, 'about the human desire to discover or invent strategies for outwitting time.' He had by this time been living and writing in the Haut Savoie for some years and it was this personal embrace of what seemed to be a more elemental and whole experience of life and its rhythms that made his relationship to our series so pertinent.

Much of my own childhood had been spent on a farm in the English home counties and there was always a feeling of holding on against odds that would eventually do for us, which they did when my father had a stroke and went bankrupt. The challenge for me has always been how to transform a kind of valedictory sadness for the lost farming culture into a forward-looking embrace of what life is becoming. I felt this about John's stories of the threatened peasant communities of the Haut Savoie, in the way they expressed a desire to hold on to the simple and elemental labouring life through a direct relationship with nature – without nostalgia or romance.

We spent ten deep winter days filming with John at his house in Mieussy. The blanket of snow outside heightened our sense of being archetypal listeners, gathered round the hearth of the storyteller at the dead time of year. In fact, the stories that John told for the film were written and delivered on the hoof – a just-in-time approach to film-making that suited Mike's improvisatory approach. Stories.

YES

by Sally Potter

For many years I had been a distant admirer of John Berger's work. *Ways of Seeing* proposed a way of thinking about looking at the world which influenced so many of us. I felt too shy to contact him directly to tell him of my admiration but was warmed by his writings and I felt I 'knew' him by osmosis. Then one day a letter arrived from him, about *The Tango Lesson*, which he has seen in Paris and liked. Astonished, honoured, humbled, I wrote back, and some weeks later I went to dinner with him and Nella Bielski in Paris. Apart from the good food and delicious conversation there was a moment in the evening that left an indelible impression. John's son, Yves, arrived with some of his paintings rolled up under his arm. With John's encouragement he showed them to those of us present. The paintings curled upwards because of how they had been carried, and so John knelt down in front of Yves and held down the lower edge of each painting for as long as we looked at it. He was on his knees for a good half hour and it seemed longer. It was an image of humility, graphically and movingly expressed.

I told him about my idea for a new film and he was encouraging. With trepidation, some weeks later I called him. Would he read something and tell me what he thought? 'Why not come over to Geneva,' he said, 'and read it to me? How about tomorrow? I will meet you at the airport . On my motorbike.' 'Oh yes, oh good.' I said, laughing a little shrilly, and trembling inwardly with a mixture of fear and excitement. But when we were speeding along the icy motorway at 100 mph, and I was leaning into his back to shield myself from the snow and wind, I thought: at this speed and in these hands, I can only trust.

That afternoon in the cosy safety of his and Beverly's house in the Haute Savoie, I read aloud the verses I had written that later became *YES*. John laughed and gestured and sighed in ways that have since become familiar; and demonstrated his concentrated, focused and utterly generous way of listening. He had 'framed' what I had written with the complicity of his attention. My cloud of self-doubt lifted. We talked animatedly until the early hours of the morning; cinema, politics, France, exile, stories after stories. The next day we moved around on bits of card the scenes I had written. 'There!' he said, once it seemed to move speedily as a narrative; 'Shumacher-esque!' More crinkle-eyed joyous laughter. A year later, when I had sent him a completed draft or two - or three - to read, it had become, 'the fucking script'. 'It's there already!' he said. You don't need to change it any more.' But my tinkering changes were partly in response to the usual 'no's from financers, (and in particular, the UKFC.) And then, when the money raising business was in full, tragic, mode (as it always seems to be for a while… one catastrophe after another, broken promises and unbearable contracts… it seems it will never happen) and a

we were speeding along the icy motorway at 100 mph, and I was leaning into his back to shield myself from the snow and wind, I thought: at this speed and in these hands, I can only trust.

kindly word from him brought tears; he said, 'There. Have a hot bath. And tomorrow we shall go to the market. You will look at the colours of vegetables. And the film will be made, you will see.'

Throughout this process I was well aware that I was one of many people looking to John for his beady eyes and generous ear; his beautifully shaped words of encouragement, for his particular level of engagement with ideas, his own and those of others - no distinction made, no rights of 'ownership' - and that he was also busily in mid-flow, in his own writings. I offered whatever I could in exchange for what I felt he gave to me, and he insisted on treating me as a peer, though I felt him to be a curious mixture of dear friend, mentor, wise elder, icon and playmate. But in the dark hours, even to think of his ready laugh, his unbroken record of artistic and political integrity, his alliance with the outcasts and oddities, the forgotten and the downtrodden, and his dedication to the job of thinker and artist, was always energising.

> Desire, as shown in your film, is the offer – from one body to another – of a reprieve from the persistent pain of life. When the offer is accepted and reciprocated, the reprieve and its promise covers both parties for a while.

I suspect that, in addition to his known and named collaborations, his is a hidden presence behind the evolution of many people's work, with his many subtle and unquantifiable contributions secretly present. For he has the genius not only of continuous fresh thinking, of never standing still in his own work, always moving on, always developing; but also - and unusually - the genius of appreciation of other peoples work as well, and of the deep and sometimes painful processes involved in making it. This is why he is such an extraordinary critic, for he sees what is there in a piece of work and can tease out its hidden levels for others; becoming their guide into its secret labyrinths. It also makes him an inestimable friend; and an inspiration to every writer, filmmaker or artist aspiring to the condition of his generosity of spirit, his level of achievement, and his pursuit of excellence. The latter not for its own sake, necessarily, (though that too) but because the honed, the worked, the far-reaching is both pleasurable and necessary as we grope our way through the mediocre and the careless.

John's work, and his interactions with others, help us to remember that this precious life, the work we can contribute to it, and the way we can choose to live it, minute to minute, needs to be honoured, fully awake. His collaborative instinct reminds us that we need each other in work and in play; that we are in it together - this messy struggle - and that it all matters. Everything. Each gesture, each meal, each painting, poem or film, each conversation or encounter an opportunity for celebration, an opportunity to learn, an opportunity to give.

*

From a letter on *Yes*, written by John Berger to Sally Potter

Yes. A film that irrefutably deserves its title. A film of affirmation. Which is not the same as a story with a happy ending.

Its storytelling, its narration, has chosen its own method. Again and again it proceeds through glances, hints, innuendos to arrive at a dénouement, a stripping away, a

nakedness. The nakednesses, to which the narration leads, are every time surprising. (As they are in life, when the one looking is attentive. Dress renders us similar, nakedness renders each of us incomparable.)

The places, the locations, are like characters, and the camera moves, all the while, around and in and through them with the same curiosity with which the cleaner examines and explains the house in which she's working. If the places in this story become characters, what is the scene? The arena of world politics today, nothing less, is the scene – and, above it, the sky to which everyone, at one moment or other, prays.

Desire, as shown in your film, is the offer – from one body to another – of a reprieve from the persistent pain of life. When the offer is accepted and reciprocated, the reprieve and its promise covers both parties for a while.

Wounds and desire – after a certain age – are inseparable. (or perhaps at all ages? I suddenly remember being four!) The reprieve is a reminder of the grace – as distinct from the cruelty of nature. Isn't this why love poetry in all cultures refers so often to the beauties of nature?

Alain Tanner
Feature Film Collaborations

JONAH WHO WILL BE 25 IN THE YEAR 2000

The (film's) two quotations (from Rousseau) set up the psycho-political guideposts of *Jonah Who Will Be 25 in the Year 2000*: on the one hand, an implacable condemnation of human society as it is; on the other, a decision to act as if the game's not up, as if the future could be better, as if a new generation might do better.

"We have nicknamed our characters the 'little prophets', first because their prophecies are little, and second because they themselves are not conscious of being prophets in the traditional sense of the term. They never announce their prophecies, which only exist for them at the individual and existential level... The danger of the great prophecies is megalomania and the absence of scruples..." Alain Tanner

The political musings in *Jonah...* are as diverse as the thoughts of the characters. No one has an integrated theory, an ideology, or certitude; yet no one but Max even feigns cynicism, and not even Max withdraws completely. Political observations crop up unsystematically - during an explanation of Tantric sex or an argument about an alternative school or a decision to take a job; while making an onion tart, posing for a mural painting, or naming a baby; in a snippet of newsreel footage or a voice-over quotation. They include ingenious riffs on time, dialectics, prophesy, revolution, and history. Take, for example, the extraordinary sausage scene which, I'd wager, no one who's seen *Jonah...* ever forgets.

Another scene explains the title of the film. Seven of the main characters are having dinner together when Mathilde announces that she and Mathieu are going to have another child. Everyone suggests a name. Mathieu likes Emile, "because of Jean-Jacques." Marcel proposes Jonah. "He fell from the ship, from the beautiful ship of fools we navigate on." Jonah strikes everyone as the right name. As Marco puts it (actually, he sings it), "the whale of history will spit out Jonah who will be twenty-five in the year 2000. That's the time left for us to help him get off the shit-pile."

When Cahiers du Cinema asked Tanner about the relationship of *Jonah...* to "the survivors of '68, of the shipwreck," he responded that 'the events' of May 1968 had much less importance than the after-effects. The events "brought out hopes and caused hidden desires to flower which have remained on the surface ever since. And that's what it is about, rather than the fate of the 'shipwrecked'." The hopes and desires at the heart of *Jonah* - dignity in work, education for democratic citizenship, environmental stewardship of the planet, non-material fulfilment - still occupy the democratic left; we're still living in the extended aftermath of the sixties... I can't think of a movie since *Jonah...* that has more successfully portrayed humane interconnectedness within a community without going sentimental. Tanner and Berger achieved a uniquely successful mix of serious ideas and story. In short, *Jonah...*, which turns twenty-eight in the year 2004, has barely aged.

Extracts from *Jonah After the Year 2000* by Joanne Barkan (published in *Dissent*, Winter 2004).

Scene 9 *Class at Geneva High School. The students, boys and girls, are about sixteen or seventeen years old. The principal of the high school introduces Marco, the new history teacher.*

The Principal I would like to introduce your new history teacher, Mr. Marco Perly, who beginning today is replacing

In agricultural societies, men believed that time consisted simply of cycles, of seasons. Each winter solstice contained the same moment. An individual grew old of course, but that was simply because he wore himself out: he was the fuel which made the machine of the seasons go.

Mr. Genthod who, as you know, has just retired. Please give him a nice welcome.

The principal leaves. Marco, who has been holding a suitcase, puts it down on the desk and opens it. He takes out a long piece of sausage, a small block, a cleaver and a metronome, all of which he shows to the amused and surprised students.

Marco Never forget that my father is a butcher and that my mother sings light opera very well.

Laughter. He lays the sausage on the cutting block and flourishes the cleaver, then sets the metronome going.

Marco Would someone like to come and cut the sausage? In time with the metronome ...

A boy rushes forward and begins to cut the sausage. Screams and laughter from the class.

Marco Good, that's enough for now.

The boy stops. Marco picks up a few pieces of the cut sausage.

Marco So these are the pieces of history. What should we call them? Hours? Decades? Centuries? It's all the same and it never stops. The sausage is eaten with mashed potatoes. Is time a sausage? Darwin thought so, even though the stuffing changed from one end of the sausage to the other. Marx thought that someday everyone would stop eating sausage. Einstein and Max Planck tore the skin off the sausage which from then on lost its shape. What is a sausage skin made of?

A Girl Pig's intestine.

Marco Very good. Now let's look at the sausage that hasn't been cut up yet. You can see creases, folds. And that's what I want to talk to you about. What are time's folds made of?

In agricultural societies, men believed that time consisted simply of cycles, of seasons. Each winter solstice contained the same moment. An individual grew old of course, but that was simply because he wore himself out: he was the fuel which made the machine of the seasons go. Capitalism will supply the idea of time-as-highway. Highway of the sun, the highway of progress. The idea of progress was that the conquerers hadn't simply won a battle, but that they had been chosen and designated because they were superior beings. Their superiority would inevitably span the cycles and seasons. It transformed them into cork-screws of which they, the conquerers, were the tip. And with that tip they opened the bottles of the lesser cultures, one after another. They drank until their thirst was quenched and tossed aside the bottles, assuring themselves that they would break. This was a new kind of violence. The arrow or the sword had previously killed, but what killed now was the verdict of history. The history of the conquerers of course. With this new violence arose a new fear among the conquerers: the fear of the past, fear of the lesser beings in their broken bottles.

Ah! If only the past could one day overtake the conquerers, it would certainly show as little pity as they themselves had shown. During the nineteenth century, this fear of the past was transformed rationally into scientific law. Time then became a road without curves. The length of the road was a terrifying abstraction, but abstractions don't take revenge. From that point on the thinkers of the nineteenth century opted for the fear of thought while eliminating the fear of the savage and his arrows. And their roads had boundaries. Absolutely regular. Millions of years divided into eras, into dates, into days and into hours of work to punch in on the time-clock. Like sausage.

*

LA SALAMANDRE

La Salamandre uses its satire of Swiss bureaucracy and materialism as the springboard for a much broader moral comedy. To begin with, its heroine is a universal misfit, an intuitive rebel who – as played with irresistible fecklessness by Bulle Ogier – would be out of place in any organised, materialist society. Secondly, the film's comic and aesthetic tensions derive from a conflict between form and spontaneity

LE MILIEU DU MONDE

For Tanner, it seems that *Le Milieu du Monde* was a turning point. He has admitted to a 'longstanding dislike of the ritual of filmic narration', and in the earlier films *Charles Mort ou Vif* and *La Salamandre* there were 'intuitive' attempts to interrupt the narrative flow, or at least break it down into small units… *Le Milieu du Monde*, however, consists of a number of systematic strategies which call into question the established codes of narrative… (and) the actual break with (his) previous work comes at the level of the articulation of shots… he has fashioned an appropriate aesthetic for the ideological concern that John Berger brings to the collaboration.

Le Milieu du Monde provides something of a well-stocked Berger portmanteau, containing themes from his art criticism, fiction and political writings. For instance, the figure of Adriana recalls certain Italian motifs from the novel *G.*, while as an immigrant worker she becomes something of a female footnote to the all-male ethos of *A Seventh Man*. More generally, the ideological framework on which the film is constructed resumes Berger's earlier emphasis on the bankruptcy of European bourgeois society, its self-delusion and bland rapacity…

The stultification and destruction of personal life is seen as inevitable under Capitalism: Paul cannot change because he is a part which denies change, he can only express hopes and fantasies. By contrast, Adriana's strength is that 'she knew what she didn't want and this enabled her to make a decision.' Although exploited by the system, she does not belong to it, she retains control over herself, her body and her emotions. The merit of *Le Milieu du Monde* lies in its determination to be lucid and responsible in unmasking dominant ideology, while paying attention to the ideological operations of the film itself.

Ian Christie, extracted from *Monthly Film Bulletin*, August 1977

which informs not just its social/political 'message' but its whole shape and style. The device of the off-screen narrator to provide an infallibly tidy framework for the story is introduced early in the film, only to be burlesqued later, while the film's length offends all the ideas of tight narrative unity set up by the 'mystery' expectations of the early scenes.

Most significantly, Pierre and Paul, endeavouring to fit Rosemonde's story into the ready compartment of a TV documentary, find not only that the girl's answers complicate rather than illuminate their inquiry, but that she begins to shape their lives as much as they had intended to structure hers. In a consumer society with its monotonous demand for the finished product, Pierre, Paul and Rosemonde all fail to deliver results. Morally, however, each learns from the episode: Pierre and Paul by discovering that human beings are not pliable subject matter for the artist or journalist; Rosemonde by finding a rationale for her previously futile sense of rebellion ("people hate my independence", she tells Paul. "They try to break me down. No one wants me the way I am."). The film's concern with spontaneity reflects the importance of being true to oneself, of not simply doing what is expected.

Nigel Andniss, extracted from *Monthly Film Bulletin*, March 1973

Another Way of Telling
Views on Photography

by John Christie

In 1988 I managed, after much persistence, to get an independent commission from the BBC to photograph and direct a series of films based on *Another Way of Telling* - John Berger and Jean Mohr's meditation on the nature and practice of photography. I'd first contacted John out of the blue three years earlier to hopefully get his agreement on the project and something, perhaps my enthusiasm - because we didn't know each other then, had persuaded him to go along with the idea that a series could be made. To my surprise he gave me the television rights to the book.

While thinking about how to bring the different elements of the book to the screen, John sent me a letter and in it he suggested a subtitle for the series - *100 Postcards About Photography*. It was the clue I needed. Their ideas, theories and stories could be divided into long and short postcards and in this way the various elements of the book would interweave in the films; John Berger's photographic theories and analysis, Jean Mohr's practical photography and stories plus the pair of them talking about their work together on books such as *A Fortunate Man* and *A Seventh Man*. In early 1988 the BBC gave the go-ahead and at the last minute a fourth element was added in the shape of a photographic workshop that John had already agreed to take part in to test out some of the ideas outlined in *Another Way of Telling*. To try to discover, for example, with the help of a group of photographers, if it is possible to construct, without a supporting text, a purely photographic narrative.

This workshop was to be held in a village in the north of Finland, just outside the Arctic Circle, a place, in May and June, of almost continuous daylight. I travelled there before the filming, with my producer Anna Ridley, to check out the location. It was a beautiful area of lakes, fast flowing rivers and pine forests. The local children were on holiday and we had the village school as our workshop headquarters and log cabins by the lake for accommodation. The place was almost completely deserted - except, unfortunately for millions of mosquitoes. The Finnish owner of the site showed us around, I think still not really believing his luck that anyone would actually come here at the height of the mosquitoe season. He said we could have any log cabin we wanted along the lakeside and make full use of the site facilities which included some large, strangely shaped, rowing boats. When I asked him about the boats he told me that they were generally used for "shooting the rabbits". I imagined a strange Finnish sport, killing rabbits with a rifle, perhaps from a moving boat while the creatures ran through the forest or drank at the water's edge. I asked him if it was difficult, "Yes, very difficult". "Is it a popular sport in Finland?" I asked. "Yes, very popular". And so on. I was curious but every question was reasonably answered. It was a few days later that it became clear that he meant rapids and not rabbits.

Once the sixteen photographers arrived language difficulties faded because photography became the common purpose. John himself had ridden up on his motorbike from France to the location and many of the photographers too, travelled there by bike. There seemed from the beginning a great rapport between John and the group and for me working with them all for the eight-day workshop was a very rewarding experience. When we weren't filming I sat in on the sessions in the school hall where the day's photographs were projected (they used a Polaroid instant slide system) and the photo-sequences discussed. Every evening there was good food, talk, vodka and the obligatory sauna, then eventually bed in the early hours of the morning, the sun just touching the horizon before beginning to rise again.

After Finland our small crew travelled to Geneva to film Jean Mohr's contribution and to the Haute Savoie for more pieces with John before returning to London where over the next three months I had to cut over thirty hours of shot material down into four half-hour programmes. In August, as I settled down to editing, John sent me a letter with some thoughts on the films, "(that they should have)...a kind of poetry, a brevity, an "inconsequential" style which continually allows life to filter in and out of the photography. As if we were crossing quicksand with a poacher who knows where to put each foot...!"

I hope in *Another Way of Telling* we managed to follow the poacher at least some of the way.

LET THE VISIBLE CONNECT

SEQUENCE
echo
visual correspondence
contrast
spatial closeness
dream metaphor
consequence
attraction

Play Me Something

by Timothy Neat

When *Play Me Something* (1989) was shown at the ISAI Conference, in Belfast in September 2002, it was the film's first public showing for seven years. I viewed it almost as a stranger. I enjoyed it. It had measure and poetry. Certain things stuck out.

First, the film has innocence, mystery and primitive force. It stands far back from the cutting edge of film technology. It is not baroque, rococo or showy, not large in scale: it has the awkwardness, the naivety, the endeavour of an early work – not so much an early work by its authors, as an early product of a new school, movement or style…Its use of form and image is realist but the result is a strange amalgam of magic, imagination, dialectic and poetry. What conceit.

Second, John Berger, the storyteller, has a magnetic screen presence that is more memorable than I had realised. He is not so much an actor as the real thing! John's story, taken from his *Once in Europa* collection, has been more changed and transformed – into a new film-creature – than I had presumed; though John's mind imprints the whole film – just as his 'voice' powers those vaporetti we see ploughing the Venetian canals.

Third, Hamish Henderson, the electrician-shaman-singer, who conjures the storyteller into the film (and the airport

waiting room), has a far more important role in the narrative than I had previously, consciously, realised – artistically and ideologically. He is the puppet master, he links Scotland and Italy: he is the deep and the banana-skin. At the end of the film, only he returns across the Barra beach from whence he came – with his horse, his cart, his load of scrap, the foul rag-and-bone shop of the heart: the others fly out or get on with their lives. As Estragon, says of the much-abused Lucky, in *Waiting for Godot*, 'he's all mankind!'.

Finally, the film's photographic stills are wonderful. They are briefly signalled at the beginning of John's story – then resolutely held back until they dominate the long slow climax of the film. Jean Mohr, a long time partner of John's, was the perfect photographer for our purpose. John Ruskin wrote that the true artist has done nothing until he has forgotten himself – something like that – and there is truth in it.

At the end of the showing my own feeling was that *Play Me Something* is a good and important film. It nurtures that imagination that has been such an important part of our better human being from Palaeolithic to modern times. And I thought of the Ice Man dying high in the Alps, and shimmering across the plain, the Queen of Cities floating on the sea.

12 August 2002

by Milena Trivier

In the summer of 2002, I went with my father to the building site where they were demolishing the stables of the chateau de Méant. I had been lent a video camera with a tripod. Holidays are a bit boring over here.

So, even if I had to wake up early, very early... For two months, I had been filming the movement of the men recovering stone arches, beams and whatever materials they could sell. At the beginning of August, there was nothing left to destroy but the north gable, a tower until then inaccessible, because of its height and the layout of the buildings.

MILENA TRIVIER FILM

English translation of John Berger's voice over

Milena? You're there? Milena? It's John here. You must be in the cutting-room. If I shut my eyes, I can see some of the demolition sequences.

In life I try not to shut my eyes before events, try not to look away. When I was young I couldn't bear the sight of blood. I'd keel over and pass out. Then, bit by bit, I tried to deal with it - the desire to look away. And I discovered something: facing a hard event is a double action: you are witnessing whatever is happening at the moment and you're learning something that'll come in handy. The present is relieved (a little) by the future!

I began to visit slaughterhouses in the cities of Europe as others visited their cathedrals. Sometimes I too prayed.

Today I see - despite the opaque screens of misinformation - the violence being globally inflicted by the rich on the poor. This, I'd say, is the first truth concerning our new century.

I see the present suffering of those who are resisting and, looking, I try to learn for the future how better to join them in their constant fights.

If I shut my eyes I'd fall into the ever-increasing panic of the rich. Let's look, open-eyed …

The Spectre of Hope

by Paul Carlin

If my memory serves me correctly, the title *The Spectre of Hope* was John's, referring to Sebastiao Salgado's portraits of children that conclude our film, "… each one a spectre of hope."

At the end of 1999, my producer Colin McCabe and I met with John and Sebastiao to discuss ways of making the film. The book *Migrations* had not yet been published and so Sebastiao referred to rough photocopies to describe the stories behind his pictures. There was a sense of bafflement about him as he moved from picture to picture: the result of six years' work in forty-six countries. It was the scale of the problem: country after country, he had photographed people driven from their homes into overcrowded cities by the charade of economic success or left behind to die of hunger and disease. These images of suffering were different to the usual over-familiar litany of facts and dismay in the media, because they allowed us to look and imagine, for an instant, what it might be like to be there ourselves. The experience was overwhelming: we were people looking at people.

Sebastiao suggested that John should interview him for the film. The following year in May, we met again at John's home in the Alps. The film was expected to take four days to shoot. On the first day, we set up the camera in John's kitchen and two days later without having moved it, the filming was complete. John's discussion with Sebastiao was intense, both men exposing their passions, doubts and above all their resistance to indifference.

Sebastiao's pictures helped us to see what we didn't want to see, and John's words made Sebastiao's pictures more visible.

Selected Filmography

The following contains films, documentaries and television programmes written by, presented by or significantly featuring John Berger and his work. It does not include many of the interviews, brief contributions or discussion appearances he has made. See relevant articles for coverage of the most important works.

Feature Films

- The Salamander
- The Middle of the World
- Jonah Who Will Be 25 in the Year 2000
- Play Me Something
- Walk Me Home
- The Three Lives of Lucie Cabrol (filmed stage production)

Series

- Monitor: a number, including 'Giacometti', 'Frisco Ten Hat', 'Picasso', 'Why Leger?' 'Release: De Stijl', 'Le Facteur Cheval', 'Artist from Moscow', '10,000 Days, 93,000 Hours, 33 Years of Effort', 'La Ville à Chandigarh.'
- Tomorrow Couldn't Be Worse
- Drawn from Life
- Ways of Seeing
- About Time
- Another Way of Telling

Television Documentaries

- A Fortunate Man
- Germinal
- Pig Earth
- All the Women You Are
- Parting Shots from Animals
- A Telling Eye
- The Spectre of Hope

Participations

- 2nd House: An Artist's Story
- Voices: to Tell a Story; with Susan Sontag
- Writers in Conversation; with Lisa Appignanesi
- Face to Face; with Jeremy Isaacs
- Huw Wheldon, by His Friends
- Borderlines
- Time and Light: a Film about Photographs
- His Name Was Tyler
- In Conversation with Michael Silverbladtt
- In Conversation with Michael Ondaatje
- 12 August 2002
- I Send You This Cadmium Red
- Titian
- Art, Poetry and Particle Physics
- Snapshots
- Crumbling Houses

The Black Dwarf

Vol. 13 Number 1   JUNE 1968   FORTNIGHTLY 1s

REVOLUCION SI!

John Berger

The people of three continents are involved in a struggle which they will never abandon until they have achieved their freedom: not the nominal freedom of independent States, but the freedom for which all others so far imagined have been a preparation: the freedom from exploitation. When they have achieved this freedom—and at the longest it will be within a century—they will produce art unimaginable by us today.   Unimaginable by us today because the freedom they win may change the condition of man.

Turn to back page

War Against Terrorism or A Terrorist War?

by John Berger

When on September 11, 2001 I watched the videos on television, I was instantly reminded of August 6th 1945. We in Europe heard the news of the bombing of Hiroshima on the evening of the same day.

The immediate correspondences between the two events include a fireball descending without warning from a clear sky, both attacks being timed to coincide with the civilians of the targeted city going to work in the morning, with the shops opening, with children in school preparing their lessons. A similar reduction to ashes, with bodies, flung through the air, becoming debris. A comparable incredulity and chaos provoked by a new weapon of destruction being used for the first time - the A-bomb sixty years ago, and a civil airliner last autumn. Everywhere at the epicentre, on everything and every body, a thick pall of dust.

The differences of context and scale are of course enormous. In Manhattan the dust was not radioactive. In 1945 the United States had been waging a full-scale, three year old war with Japan. Both attacks, however, were planned as announcements.

Watching either, one knew that the world would never again be the same; the risks everywhere, to which life was heir, had been changed on the morning of a new unclouded day.

The bombs dropped on Hiroshima and Nagasaki announced that the United States was henceforth the supreme armed power in the world. The attack of September 11th announced that this power was no longer guaranteed invulnerability on its home ground. The two events mark the beginning and end of a certain historical period.

Concerning President Bush's riposte to September 11th, his so-called "War against terrorism", which was first baptised Infinite Justice, and then renamed Enduring Freedom, concerning this riposte the most trenchant and anguished comments and analyses I have come across have been made and written by United States citizens. The accusation of "anti-Americanism" against those of us who adamantly oppose the present decision-makers in Washington is as short-sighted as the policies in question. There are countless anti-American U.S. citizens, with whom we are in solidarity.

There are also many U.S. citizens who support these policies, including the 60 intellectuals who signed a statement which set out to define what is a "just" war in general, and why in particular the operation Enduring Freedom in Afghanistan, and the ongoing war against terrorism, are justified.

They argued that the moral justification for a just war is when its purpose is to defend the innocent against evil. They quoted St. Augustine. They added that such a war must respect as far as possible the immunity of non-combatants.

If their text is read innocently (and of course it was not written either spontaneously or innocently), it suggests a patient gathering of erudite, quietly-spoken experts, with access to a great library (and perhaps, between sessions, a swimming pool) who have the time and quiet to reflect, to discuss their hesitations, and finally to come to an agreement and offer their judgment. And it suggests that this meeting took place somewhere in a mythic 6 Star hotel (access only by helicopter) in its own spacious grounds, surrounded by high walls with guards and checkpoints. No contact whatsoever between thinkers and the local populations. No chance meetings. As a result, what really happened in history and what is happening today beyond the walls of the hotel is unadmitted and unknown. Isolated De Luxe Tourist Ethics.

Return to the summer of 1945. Sixty-six of Japan's largest cities had been burnt down by napalm bombing. In Tokyo a million civilians were homeless and 100,000 people had died. They had been, according to Major General Curtis Lemay, who was in charge of the fire bombing operations, "scorched and boiled and baked to death". President Franklin Roosevelt's son and confidant said that the bombing should continue "until we have destroyed about half the Japanese civilian population". On July 18 the Japanese Emperor telegraphed President Truman, who had succeeded Roosevelt, and once again asked for peace. The message was ignored.

A few days before the bombing of Hiroshima, Vice

Admiral Radford boosted that "Japan will eventually be a nation without cities - a nomadic people".

The bomb, exploding above a hospital in the centre of the city, killed 100,000 people instantly, 95% of them civilians. Another 100,000 died slowly from burns and the effects of radiation.

"Sixteen hours ago," President Truman announced, "an American airplane dropped one bomb on Hiroshima, an important Japanese army base."

One month later the first uncensored report - by the intrepid Australian journalist Wilfred Burchett - described the cataclysmic suffering he encountered after visiting a makeshift hospital in the city.

General Groves, who was the military director of the Manhattan Project for planning and manufacturing the bomb, hastily reassured Congressmen that radiation caused no "undue suffering" and that "in fact, they say it is a very pleasant way to die".

In 1946 the U.S. Strategic Bombing Survey came to the conclusion that "Japan would have surrendered even if atomic bombs had not been dropped...."

To describe a course of events as briefly as I have, is of course to over-simplify. The Manhattan Project was started in 1942 when Hitler was triumphant and there was the risk that researchers in Germany might manufacture atomic weapons first. The U.S. decision, when this risk no longer existed, to drop two atomic bombs on Japan, needs to be considered in the shadow of the atrocities committed by Japanese armed forces across South-East Asia, and the surprise attack on Pearl Harbor in December 1941. There were U.S. commanders and certain scientists working on the Manhattan Project who did their best to delay or argue against Truman's fateful decision.

Yet finally, when all was said and done, the unconditional surrender of Japan on August 14th could not have been, and was certainly not, celebrated as the longed-for victory. There was an anguish at the centre of it, and a blindness which blinded.

POSTER BY ANTHONY BARNETT : 50CM X 75CM

Working with John
by Anthony Barnett

Have I ever worked with John? I don't think so, it has never seemed like work to me. Struggled, for sure, and disagreed, laughed often. But not worked.

The first time I encountered him, we were brought together in a Soho restaurant by Clive Goodwin, the owner of the *Black Dwarf*, an occasionally fortnightly paper whose aim was to kindle the spirit of revolution across the land. It was 1970. I had been enthusing about Antonioni's film *Zabriskie Point*. But the line on the left was to decry and condemn the movie. (Perhaps because the film prefigured the nihilism and futility of callow gauchism, though I don't claim that was what I saw in it at the time.)

The meeting was a set-up, in a way a sort of civilised show-trial. The lunch table was arranged so that I was placed opposite the great man (whose art criticism had illuminated my boyhood reading). He was currently making a rare visit to London. He arrived. There were at least six others. Could I defend my view? I have no memory of how I praised the culprit movie. There was a pause. For the first time, John looked at me with his famous gaze. The pause continued. Very intently, so did the gaze. Time was taken to internalise and weigh my words. "Yes", pause, "Yes, you are right!"

"Damn!" - I vividly recall being very annoyed - I wanted an argument!

It was two years before we met again. Shortly after that, with great and spontaneous generosity, he helped me to recover from a crisis and we began our friendship. Later, by insisting, and it was quite a campaign of persuasion, that he would be welcomed as a Fellow at the TNI, I helped him when "the black force" as he described it, weighed upon his shoulder.

ORLANDO LETELIER

1932 - 1976

Appointed Chile's Socialist Minister of Defence in 1973. Marched from his Ministry at gunpoint during the coup, 11th September 1973. Taken to Dawson Island, tortured, his fingers broken (he played the guitar). Released a year later. Goes to the USA. Elected Director of the Transnational Institute of Amsterdam and Washington, 1976. Calls for the downfall of the Chilean Junta. Blown up in his car in Washington DC by Cuban exiles acting under the orders of the present rulers of Chile.

Once I will visit you
he said
in your mountains
today
assassinated
blown to pieces
he has come to stay
he lived in many places
and he died everywhere
in this room
he has come between the pages
of open books
there's not a single apple
on the trees
loaded with fruit this year
which he has not counted
apples the colour of gifts
he faces death no more
there's not a precipice
over which his corpse
has not been hurled
the silence of his voice
tidy and sweet as the leaf of a beech
will be safe in the forest
I never heard him speak
in his mother tongue
except when he named the names
of patriots
the clouds race over the grass
faster than sheep
never lost
he consulted the compass of his heart
always accurate
took bearings from the needle of Chile
and the eye of Santiago
through which he has now passed.

Before the fortress of injustice
he brought many together
with the delicacy of reason
and spoke there
of what must be done
amongst the rocks
not by giants
but by women and men
they blew him to pieces
because he was too coherent
they made the bomb
because he was too fastidious
what his assassins whisper to themselves
his voice could never have said
afraid of his belief
in history
they chose the day
of his murder.

He has come
as the season turns
at the moment of the blood red rowenberry
he endured the time without seasons
which belongs to the torturers
he will be here too
in the spring
every spring
until the seasons returning
explode
in Santiago.

John Berger
Sept. 1976

Transnational Institute, Paulus Potterstraat, Amsterdam

Vail Printers Ltd., King's Cross, London

INTRODUCTION
& LITERATURE
FILM &
TELEVISION
VISUAL ART
PERFORMANCE

John Berger trained as an artist and his first published writing for *Tribune* and then *The New Statesman* was as a commentator on visual art. It was here, in his trenchant, provocative and engaged columns and articles, that he set out his stall on the relationship between visual culture and power. More specifically, his reading of both historically established artists and of contemporary makers saw him refuse to remove the artefacts produced – canvases, drawings, sculptures – from the environments, whether economic, social or political, in which they were produced. While he was not unique in this, his ability to explore complex ideas about ownership, class hierarchies and injustice around the work, while never losing sight of either the original work, its merits or its grace, saw him communicate these ideas with great dynamism and reach.

Many books and essays followed that developed this position across the entire realm of the seen world, from zoos, and the gaze of animals, to the coded oppressions of advertising. On a popular level, this can be seen to culminate in the huge impact of *Ways of Seeing*, and yet the success of this particular enquiry can sometimes obscure the richness and continuing relevance of dozens of other pieces.

But John also works as a maker in this area. He has always drawn and painted, and has opened his books to designers, notably Richard Hollis, to make their own interventions in the shared material in question. As well as designing *Ways of Seeing*, Hollis also set *A Seventh Man*, John's prophetic investigation, with Swiss photographer Jean Mohr, of Turkish migrant workers in Europe. It is with Mohr, across three extremely influential books, that John has most directly explored the shifting nature of the relationship between image and word.

This question has also been raised in a very different way in the bookworks he has made with John Christie, most significantly in *I Send You This Cadmium Red*, a dazzling investigative correspondence around colour and its cultural/historical codings.

More recent projects include shared drawing with Maggi Hambling and Marisa Camino, a moving encounter with Giacometti alongside Belgian photographer Marc Trivier and ongoing dialogues with his son Yves and daughter Katya. Testing ideas in the realm of the visual remains perhaps the way by which John continues to make his most acute readings of both the present and the past.

Jean Mohr: Photographic Collaborations
A Fortunate Man

by Jean Mohr

We had been working for more than a month, staying at the house of the doctor. He would take us around when he was visiting his patients and call us, even at night, if somebody came and rang the bell for help in one way or another. It could be psychological as well as just physical help and he would wake us up and say "I'm working, so please come down".

So, we had been doing that all the time, I had been shooting, I don't remember, maybe not much but thirty or forty rolls of black and white film, and John had been taking notes. Then we went home, home for both of us meant Geneva, and he began to write down his text and I spent a lot of time in my darkroom. One month later we met, he had his manuscript ready, I had a box with about two hundred black and white prints, eight by ten, and we exchanged our work. John looked at my pictures, I started to read his text, then suddenly he shouted, he wasn't very pleased, "You have ruined nearly all I've done". I said, "Why, what is wrong with the pictures?" and he replied, "I have been trying to describe landscapes, people, faces, it took me a long time, it was very hard, and you, with just one picture, you do much better sometimes". So I was feeling pleased and flattered, then he said "But I have to tell you that more than half of your pictures we have to forget about because both of us have made the same mistake, we have tried to do the book all by ourselves. You have tried with some abstract pictures to describe situations, what was going on in the mind of people, and that's not your business that's my business, I have to deal with that. So I want to rewrite most of my text, keeping in mind what you have done, what we'll keep, pictures describing both the context and the work of the doctor and forget about all those beautiful pictures which you may use one day in an exhibition but which have nothing to do with the book."

I accepted his point of view because I felt he was right. I still fought for some pictures that I felt were essential but in the end we agreed about the ones that were really necessary, meaning those that were exactly in counterpoint with his text, and that became the book *A Fortunate Man*.

From the BBC series 'Another Way of Telling'

JEAN MOHR

Why A Fortunate Man Matters
by Iona Heath

For me, and countless others, this is quite simply the most extraordinary book ever written about general practice. Extraordinary in that it describes the essential aspirations and transactions of general practice in a way which is instantly familiar to those of us who are engaged in practice every day; and yet it is written not by a general practitioner but by someone who simply observed from the outside. Through a great feat of empathic imagination, John Berger describes what we already know but have somehow been unable to express for ourselves. Reading *A Fortunate Man* we feel that deep resonating affirmation we experience when touched by poetry. At the same time, Jean Mohr's photographs somehow manage to show us exactly how imagination and empathy work. The achievements of John Sassall, the doctor, John Berger, the writer and Jean Mohr, the photographer all depend on intense and generous attention to the dignity and detail of faces and of eyes and of the particular tangible circumstances of individual lives. The photographs do not illustrate the text; they are an integral part of the writing, taking it beyond the limitations of words.

The book's consistent themes of continuity, recognition and solidarity are almost completely absent from all the official documentation of general practice and primary care. These attributes are easily lost in a world committed to short-term solutions and simplistic targets, but without them the humanity of both doctors and patients is diminished and the task of providing genuine care proportionately more difficult. This book helps us to defend those foundations of our work which we rediscover every day and which we know to be crucial to everything that we do.

If, in a lifetime, I was allowed to read only one book about general practice, this would be it. We owe John Berger and Jean Mohr a huge debt of gratitude not only for this enduringly wonderful book but for granting the Royal College of General Practitioners permission to publish a new edition.

I have to tell you that more than half of your pictures we have to forget about because both of us have made the same mistake, we have tried to do the book all by ourselves.

A Seventh Man

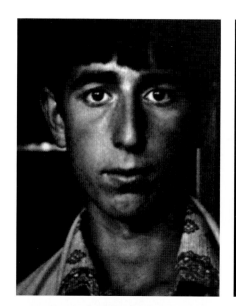

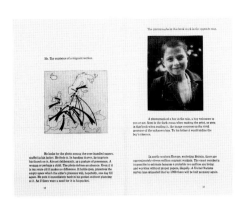

The Seventh

by Attila Jozsef

If you set out in this world,
better be born seven times.
Once, in a house on fire,
once, in a freezing flood,
once, in a wild madhouse,
once, in a field of ripe wheat,
once, in an empty cloister,
and once among pigs in a sty.
Six babies crying, not enough:
you yourself must be the seventh.

When you must fight to survive,
let your enemy see seven.
One, away from work on Sunday,
one, starting his work on Monday,
one, who teaches without payment,
one, who learned to swim by drowning,
one, who is the seed of the forest,
and one, whom wild forefathers protect,
but all their tricks are not enough:
you yourself must be the seventh.

If you want to find a woman,
let seven men go for her.
One, who gives his heart for words,
one, who takes care of himself,
one, who claims to be a dreamer,
one, who through her skirt can feel her,
one, who knows the hooks and snaps,
one, who steps upon her scarf:
let them buzz like flies around her.
You yourself must be the seventh.

If you write and can afford it,
let seven men write your poem.
One, who builds a marble village,
one, who was born in his sleep,
one, who charts the sky and knows it,
one, whom words call by his name,
one, who perfected his soul,
one, who dissects living rats.
Two are brave and four are wise;
you yourself must be the seventh.

And if all went as was written,
you will die for seven men.
One, who is rocked and suckled,
one, who grabs a hard young breast,
one, who throws down empty dishes,
one, who helps the poor to win,
one, who works until he goes to pieces,
one, who just stares at the moon.
The world will be your tombstone:
you yourself must be the seventh.

Another Way Of Telling

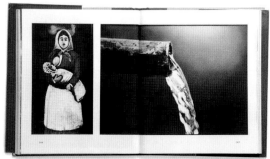

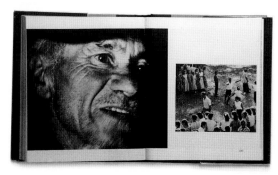

JEAN MOHR

On Design

by Richard Hollis

John taught life drawing at Chelsea School of Art in the 1950s. Teachers varied from the woolly Bonnardesque to followers of the Euston Road school, using the pencil as a plumb line and spirit level to scatter the paper with measured dots and crosses in space. John was after something else. He helped students to think and feel as well as draw. He would usher you out of the life room to ask if you understood the model's pose. "Can you sense the weight the model must feel on her hip?" To demonstrate, he exaggerated the model's stance.

Most often down to earth, he pointed out simple things otherwise overlooked. Reviewing a Tate Gallery sculpture exhibition which placed works against the wall, he was obliged to remind his readers – and the curators – that sculpture should be seen from all sides. This was in *The New Statesman*. Did John give painting lessons to the editor, Kingsley Martin? He certainly went to Lord Beaverbrook's house to advise about some paintings. In Park Lane the butler greeted him with, "may I take your hat and gloves, Sir?" It was obvious that John had neither.

John's serious interest in people from time to time stimulates something directly in his writing. When he visited Kenneth Clark in Saltwood, the encounter was transformed into an episode in *A Painter of Our Time*, a novel whose hero was inspired by the one-time Constructivist sculptor László (Peter) Peri, founder of the Association of Artists for Revolutionary Proletarian Art.

His generous championing of improbable and neglected artists has been one of John's salient aspects. It is quite independent of current taste. For him, the artist may represent something more than the art. His enthusiasm for the Russian sculptor Ernst Neizvestny has been found baffling, while his judgement can be can be sharp and surprising. In preparing *Ways of Seeing*, a Rembrandt was proposed as an illustration. John said at once, "It's not a very good painting." The others in the room were startled; the director of the television version, Mike Dibb, protested. "But just look at the arm", John replied, and he went on to convince them with further explanations. If this makes John sound decisive and categorical, that's misleading. In conversation he can seem to be only stalking the truth. He can articulate an argument over several minutes only to shake his head in exasperation with himself, ending with a smile, "No, no, no! That's quite wrong."

As I learned, this was an attitude which could extend to his writing. His novel *G.* was laid out by cutting up the galley proofs and pasting them on the pages. If a chapter ended with a few lines on a fresh page, he was asked if it could be cut back. "Of course", he said, "How many lines?"

John had planned *G.* as a book with documentary images, along the lines of André Breton's *Nadja*. This idea was abandoned, but the physical cutting and pasting of text and illustrations was the method of *Ways of Seeing* and *A Seventh Man*. John was auteur, both director and collaborator. Words and pictures were interdependent. In the same way his articles for *New Society* challenged us to search for the telling illustration, not just an image but "l'image juste". Helping us to think about the images we are making and using is where John enters people's lives.

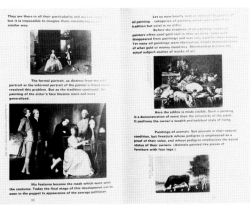

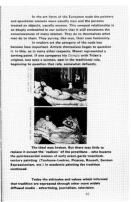

I Send You This Cadmium Red
& other book collaborations

by John Christie

One evening during the filming of *Another Way of Telling* the conversation turned from photography to books and how many books whose texts deal with the visual arts and aesthetics are in themselves, as objects, not very aesthetically pleasing - poor paper, typography, etc. I suggested to John that perhaps in the future we might produce a book together, one that would please us on all counts. In 1994 after slowly gathering the material together I designed and printed a large-format book at Circle Press of John's poems, photographs and drawings called *Pages of the Wound*. Because

of the relatively small edition (90 copies) a paperback version was suggested to Bloomsbury and published two years later. The cover image on the paperback, which looks a little like the foliage of a tree is actually the mass of reversed signatures left on the blotting paper we'd used when John was signing the original edition.

In 1997 I phoned him at his home in France and asked if this might be a good moment to begin a new project, perhaps something to do with colour, a wide enough subject, and see what would happen - maybe even end up making another film

Self-portrait 1914-18

It seems now that I was so near to that war.
I was born eight years after it ended
When the General Strike had been defeated.

Yet I was born by Very Light and shrapnel
On duck boards
Among limbs without bodies.

I was born of the look of the dead
Swaddled in mustard gas
And fed in a dugout.

I was the groundless hope of survival
With mud between my finger and thumb
Born near Abbeville.

I lived the first year of my life
Between the leaves of a pocket bible
Stuffed in a khaki haversack.

I lived the second year of my life
With three photos of a woman
Kept in a standard issue army paybook.

In the third year of my life
At 11am on November 11th 1918
I became all that was conceivable.

Before I could see
Before I could cry out
Before I could go hungry

I was the world fit for heroes to live in.

together. John liked the idea and I asked how we could begin.
"Just send me a colour" he replied. After I'd put the phone
down, this request, given that I had the whole spectrum to
choose from, didn't seem quite so easy as it had first appeared.
Over the next week or so I tried to decide which colour to
send. Then I attended the funeral of my wife's aunt, someone
I didn't really have any emotional connection with, and during
the service my attention was distracted by some red and white
carnations in a jar. When I got home I tried from memory to
find the same red in my watercolour box and settled on

By John Berger from *Pages of the Wound*

At the book launch in Barcelona, after the reading,
a woman in the audience asked why we had never
chosen grey as one of the colours. We had to explain
that almost all the colours were there because they
had presented themselves in one way or another to
us - the colour grey had never presented itself.

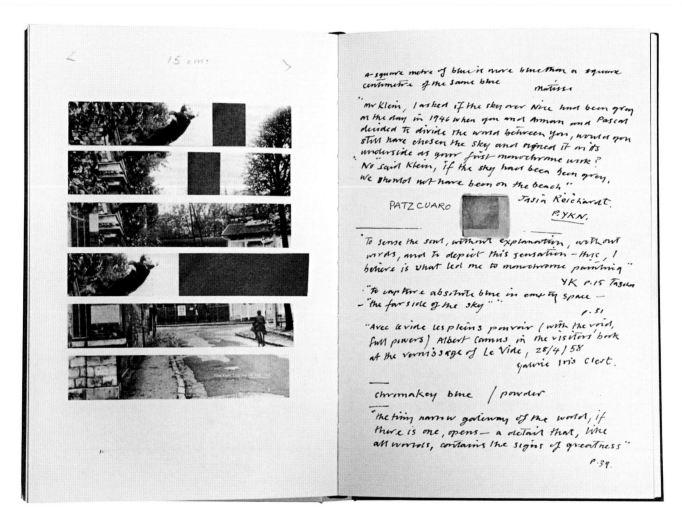

cadmium red. I painted a square of the colour on a folded
card and wrote John a letter trying describe why I had
chosen that particular red. A week later I received his reply,
written on dark red paper, in which he reacted to my letter
and the colour I'd sent him as ...*an innocent red, the red of
childhood, the red of young eyelids shut tight, the red you
saw when you did that.*

   The correspondence went on for about two years, not
continuously because various events in our lives interrupted
the flow; John wrote his novel *King* during this time, I was
away filming quite a bit and my daughter Alice was born. Very

soon after it started we settled into replying to each other in a
particular way. John would almost always send hand-written
letters, some with painted colours as part of the information,
and I would almost always, as well as a letter, make him a small
book to express ideas or thoughts that I found hard to put
into words alone. We wrote to each other about blue, brown,
black (in the disguise of darkness), yellow as a representation
of light, gold, green, mother-of-pearl, rust, varnish, saffron,
cave paintings, Matisse, Joseph Beuys, Yves Klein and many
other related things that interested us.

   In 2000, due to the energy of our mutual friend Eulalia

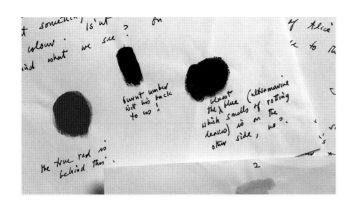

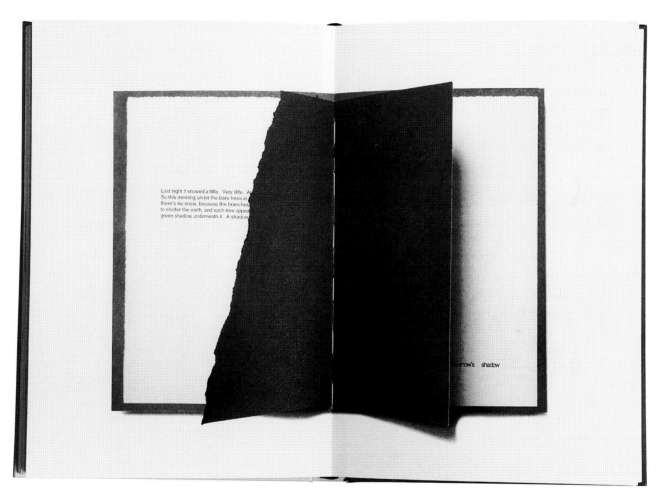

Bosch the whole correspondence became not a film but a book, published under the title *I Send You This Cadmium Red*, a phrase John plucked from that first letter I sent him. At the book launch in Barcelona, after the reading, a woman in the audience asked why we had never chosen grey as one of the colours. We had to explain that almost all the colours were there because they had presented themselves in one way or another to us, through books, quotations, exhibitions or everyday things seen in the street - the colour grey had never presented itself. The next morning we went to an exhibition of Giacometti's work at a gallery in one of Gaudi's buildings

on the Passeig de Gracia and John spotted something. It was a quote from the artist answering the question as to why his later paintings tended always to grey? Giacometti's reply, if I remember correctly, was that grey contained all colours.

Incidents like the chance encounter with a quotation about grey on the wall of an exhibition were exactly how the colours found their way into our correspondence - if grey had offered itself to us at the beginning who knows where we would have travelled to. Perhaps though it was best to begin with cadmium red, that ...innocent red of childhood - rather than grey, the mother of them all.

My Beautiful

by John Berger

The first thing to do is to look at the photos. Stop reading. Please look at them again.

You saw that they are not what they first appeared to be? They are not "reproductions" of Giacometti's sculptures, as in a good art catalogue. They do not record, they collaborate. Instead of facing the sculptures, Marc Trivier puts himself and his talent for waiting with the camera beside them. Then they all turn and advance in an Indian file. The sculptures leading and the photographs following behind, often stepping in to the same footprints.

Maybe these words can join the file.

I remember two stories. The first about Trivier, the second about Giacometti. Marc was taking photos and shifting the sculptures around a lot in order to find the place and light each one needed. Each time he carried Annette, who is only 60 cm. high, he found himself holding her tight against his chest. He couldn't keep her at arm's length, and this he found surprising.

One day somebody asked Alberto: When your sculptures finally have to leave the studio, where should they go? To a museum? And he replied: No, bury them in the earth, like that they may be a bridge between the living and the dead.

The light in the photograph of a single leg is like the light in an indoors swimming pool. I learnt to swim in such a pool in Eastbourne with my father. There was a life-belt hanging on the wall of white tiles and on it was printed Eastbourne Town Council. I think I learnt to read easily and to swim in the same year - 1931.

After 1945 Giacometti's sculptures of people (and a cat and a dog) became thinner and thinner and so it was concluded that they were on the point of disappearing. Trivier doesn't see them like that; for him they are at the point of arrival, they have just appeared. Annette arrives at the same instant as he considers her. Annette is the attention she is attracting. The truth of this has something to do with desire but it is too soon to speak of it.

Annette is persistent. She does not allow us to leave easily. She does not look at us. We have to imagine her doing so. It is partly for this that we stay.

In the Indian file I spot Katrin. Here is a photo of her. I pinned it to the wall above my working table after she died.

Katrin Cartlidge, actress. We often discussed the parts she was playing or was about to play in a film or on the stage. Each time she performed a role I had the impression she was playing one of her hundred previous lives. Her hundred very distinct lives which meant she was familiar with a hundred very distinct wounds. When she sent me an SMS she signed off with the name - Wing. It had something to do with a joke between.

About two months after her entirely unexpected death, I had the impression, when I pictured her in my mind, that she was withdrawing or had withdrawn. (I'm not sure whether this happened gradually or in a quantum leap; I suspect the latter.) She was no less present but her way of being present was altered. Previously she would be there in a particular place or context, which changed from day to day. A street market or a path through a wood, or she was asleep in a train, or she was reading out loud in a café something I'd written, or she was laughing fit to kill herself on a staircase. Now she seemed to be in several places at the same moment. No, more than that: she was at the same moment in a multitude of places or lives such as I couldn't envisage. Couldn't, not through a lack of imagination on my part, but through a lack of magnanimity. Her presence was as precise as before but it had become unlimited. Her here had become everywhere.

Sweetheart! that sounds good but it's not accurate. You're not in a position to say Here about where I am!
I should say There?
It would be better Sweetheart, or you could say here and here and here and here and here and here - and never stop!
Like a frog!
Laughter. Then words spoken quietly. (Her frequent laughter often lead to a quiet.)

The word OR implies a choice and I no longer have to choose, John I've replaced the word OR with the word AND and I love it. Isn't AND the word both Annette and I make you think of?

"AND is neither a relation nor really a conjunction, it subtends all relations, is their flow, is what allows them to overspill beyond their boundaries, beyond what can be thought of as Being, beyond One or All."

Those words are not mine but Gilles'. He loved collaborations and a multitude of voices.

Titian: Nymph and Shepherd
Letters between a daughter and father

by Katya Berger Andreadakis & John Berger

Athens

John,

I try to find an answer to the question 'What made him paint?' And I can only hear one word, coming from all the chaos of physical matter, as if from the bottom of a black well.

Desire. His desire (as befits an eminently virile painter) was, if not to cut into appearances, at least to penetrate and lose himself in the skin of things. Yet, being human and being a painter, he came up against the impossibility of doing this. The heart of nature, the animal in humans, the world's pelt can never be seized, and, above all, they are unrepeatable, unreproducible. And so, for a while, like many of his contemporaries, he used his skill to show that everything was vanity, vanitas vanitatis: beauty, wealth, art.

The women in his pictures – or rather the Titian woman, with her special simplicity and innocence – is to him a relentless reminder of his artistic impotence and defeat. Him the master! Perhaps it was women who embodied the doubt you talk about? Naked, the colours of their flesh are for drowning in. Never have the painted bodies of women demanded as much as his do, to be touched, to be pressed with the hands – as Mary Magdalene presses her hand through her hair against her own breast. Yet like all bodies in paintings across the whole world, those painted by Titian can be neither touched nor plunged into…

Love, Katya

Paris

Kut,

Vanitas vanitatis. In 1575, the Plague ravaged Venice, killing almost a third of the city's inhabitants. The old man, aged nearly a hundred, died from the Plague in 1576. As did his son. After their deaths, their house on the Biri Grande, full of pictures and precious objects, was looted. And the following year, a fire in the Ducal Palace destroyed paintings by Bellini, Veronese, Tintoretto, and the old man.

I see you today, not in the Piazza San Marco, but on the terrace of your flat in Athens. In Gyzi, where all the kitchens and bedrooms overlook one another, and the washing hangs between telephone cables and hibiscus flowers. Perhaps Athens is the antipodes of Venice? Dry, makeshift, ungovernable. A city of merchants, national heroes, where nobody dresses up…

Love, John

Triptych

By Yves Berger

She's on the point. Let's pull. He's not small and she was long overdue. A hand inside, damp, warm. Withdraw hand wet with the most beautiful dribble of dribbles. He's well placed, feet first, ready for the passage. Tie the rope above the hoof, the shin is thin and the hoof wide. Like this it's less likely to slip, yet it slips, won't hold. Not for the moment. Hang on to the rope whilst I get the loop over. Pull, tighten and now let go. You, my lady, push. The rope taut, the loop tightens. Push again Maman. We're praying, not shouting, we're red and sweating, dripping with hopes as we pull. He's too large. He comes forward then he has to draw back. He digs a hole with his head in there, he crushes his tongue, for the air is so near and so distant. A tearing apart, she moos, the tearing a sound which blinds, a cloth whose threads snap like branches. Twist the fingers round the hoof, open the passage, tuck up the skin and flex every muscle. Again pull! Again, our effort will burn up our strength. The head's out and is bigger than the neck still inside. It's red, it's blue and glistens. Blood is being diluted in the most beautiful dribbles. The rope slackens. Shin weeps. Out he comes into the air and the cold water. He has made it, alive, with us standing there, arms dangling, silly.

A page, a picture made of many pictures. The same one over and over again. It came from a photo booth. A photo booth which didn't have infinity in it's programme. Press A for Portrait. Press B for 4 IDs. Press C for? When they were young they drew back the curtain and stepped into the cabin for the fun of it and for a souvenir. Others followed, then others. How many? So many, fractions of seconds, everywhere. First flash: cheek to cheek. Second flash: kissing. When the third flash came the cabin was empty. They had opened the curtain and were laughing in the fresh air. A picture in colour, the single colour of a myriad flames dancing on the same wick. Soft to the touch. A grain of the grains of time past and time future, ever present. If it gets in your eye, you cry. If it's in your heart, it beats faster. It may contain her, him, them, whoever you choose. They want one more. Scraps of life, souvenirs of paths crossing, threaded together and chasing one another, the last pursuing the first. Some such fraction of

a second, some such instant known time and again, is permanently at the centre of our being. Its light fluctuates from one end of our lives to the other, making here and there many pictures of the same picture.

It's dark here. The night hasn't woken up yet. She's small, young and for the moment she's asleep. Her vocabulary is growing, her teeth are growing, she's growing, growing up, pink, red, white. The peaceful silence, stretched out in the dark, senses a needle enter her flesh. No more than a pinprick, ridiculous, incandescent. Then it breaks into as many screams as there are stars tonight. She howls. We tremble. It's suddenly cold. I can no longer hear anything, I hear everything. Pain splitting our bodies. Our bodies useless under the bombs of life. Heart no longer believing in the hope offered by a pair of arms, shaking in misery, broken into, sacked. How to bring calm? She is afraid, afraid of pain. We're afraid she's in pain, or worse still, that one day she'll stop feeling pain. The middle of the night, body invisible, wound lacerating. The screams reveal the total silence of the world they cross. I go to pieces. I resist without knowing it. It's over, teeth clenched on nerves. Everything forgotten. The smashed air disappears. It was only a night terror - what more normal? The night is, sometimes, bound to wake up and make our hearts pound, to deflate the illusion of peace, to hustle us to the pit of the bed where we lie hunched up, ready to leap out of our bodies and stop the lot. But it's no go, growth, all the same, goes on.

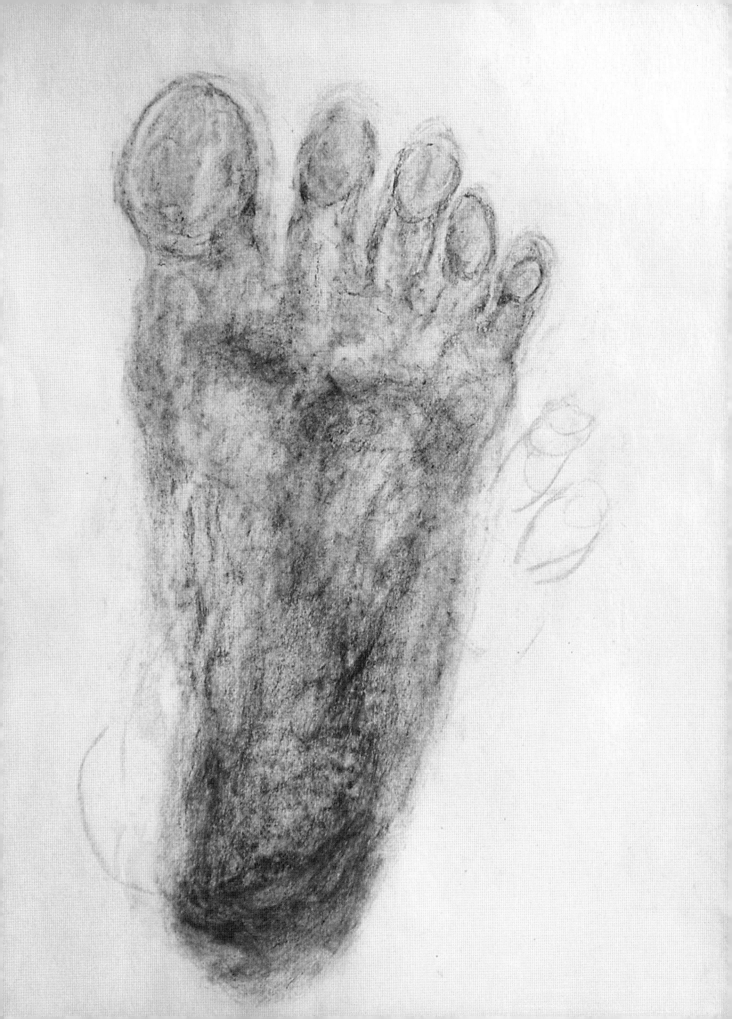

Drawing John

by Maggi Hambling

In 1994 a letter from John Berger appeared out of the blue. He had seen a bit of my work and liked it. A correspondence began, his novels and my catalogues were exchanged and then, at his Purdy Hicks drawing exhibition, we met.

John visited my studio in summer 2000, saw my drawings of Henrietta Moraes and pronounced that they should be published as a book in which he would write. And he would make it happen.

In October that year I went to stay with him in Quincy and we drew each other. My challenge was to attempt to capture something of John's intensity, his eloquent silence, his remarkable life-force.

I Would Softly Tell My Love

by John Berger

Friday

Nazim, I'm in mourning and I want to share it with you, as you shared so many hopes and so many mournings with us.

"The telegram came at night,
only three syllables:
'He is dead'."

I'm mourning my friend Juan Muñoz, a wonderful artist who died yesterday on a beach in Spain, aged 48.

I want to ask you about something which puzzles me. After a natural death, as distinct from victimisation, killing or dying from hunger, there is first the shock, unless the person has been ailing for a long while, then there is the monstrous sense of loss, particularly when the person is young -

"The day is breaking
but my room
is composed of a long night."

and there follows the pain, which says of itself that it will never end. Yet with this pain there comes surreptitiously, something else which approaches a joke but is not one, (Juan was a good joker.) something which hallucinates, a little similar to the gesture of a conjuror's handkerchief after a trick, a kind of lightness, totally opposed to what one is feeling. You recognise what I mean? Is this lightness a frivolity or a new instruction?

Five minutes after my asking you this, I received a fax from my son Yves, with some lines he had just written for Juan:

"You always appeared
with a laugh
and a new trick.

You always disappeared
leaving your hands
on our table.

You disappeared
leaving your cards
in our hands.

You will re-appear
with a new laugh
which will be a trick."

Saturday

I'm not sure whether I ever saw Nazim Hikmet. I would swear to it that I did, but I can't find the circumstantial evidence. I believe it was in London in 1954. Four years after he had been released from prison, nine years before his death. He was speaking at a political meeting held in Red Lion Square, London. He said a few words and then he read some poems. Some in English, others in Turkish. His voice was strong, calm, highly personal and very musical. But it did not seem to come from his throat - or not from his throat at that moment. It was as though he had a radio in his breast, which he switched on and off with one of his large, slightly trembling, hands. I'm describing it badly because his presence and sincerity were very obvious. In one of his long poems he describes six people in Turkey listening in the early 1940's to a symphony by Shostakovich on the radio. Three of the six people are (like him) in prison. The broadcast is live; the symphony is being played at that same moment in Moscow, several thousand kilometres away. Hearing him read his poems in Red Lion Square, I had the impression that the words he was saying were also coming from the other side of the world. Not because they were difficult to understand (they were not) , nor because they were blurred or weary (they were full of the capacity of endurance), but because they were being said to somehow triumph over distances and to transcend endless separations. The here of all his poems is elsewhere.

"In Prague a cart -
a one-horse wagon
passes the Old Jewish Cemetery
The cart is full of longing for another city,
I am the driver."

When I first read some poems by Nazim Hikmet I was in my late teens. They were published in an obscure international literary review in London, under the aegis of the British Communist Party. I was a regular reader. The Party line on poetry was crap, but the poems and stories published were often inspiring.

Even when he was sitting on the platform before he got up to speak, you could see he was an unusually large and tall man. It was not for nothing that he was nick-named "The tree with blue eyes". When he did stand up, you had the impression he was also very light, so light that he risked to become airborne.

Perhaps I never did see him, for it would seem unlikely that, at a meeting organised in London by the international Peace movement, Hikmet would have been tethered to the platform by several guy ropes so that he should remain earth-bound. Yet that is my clear memory. His words after he pronounced them rose into the sky - it was a meeting outdoors - and his body made as if to follow the words he had written, as they drifted higher and higher above the Square and above the sparks of the one-time trams which had been suppressed three or four years before along Theobald's Road.

> *"You're a mountain village*
> > *in Anatolia,*
> *you're my city,*
> > > *most beautiful and most unhappy.*
> *You're a cry for help - I mean, you're my country;*
> > *the footsteps running towards you are mine."*

Monday morning
Nearly all the contemporary poets who have counted most for me during my long life I have read in translation, seldom in their original language. I think it would have been impossible for anyone to say this before the twentieth century. Arguments about poetry being or not being translatable went on for centuries. - but they were chamber arguments like chamber music. During the twentieth century most of the chambers were reduced to rubble. New means of communication, global politics, imperialisms, world markets, etc. threw millions of people together and took millions of people apart in an indiscriminate and quite unprecedented way. And as a result the expectations of poetry changed; more and more the best poetry counted on readers who were further and further away.

> *"Our poems*
> *like milestones*
> *must line the road."*

During the twentieth century, many naked lines of poetry were strung between different continents, between forsaken villages and distant capitals. You all know it, all of you, Hikmet, Brecht, Vallejo, Atilla Jósef, Adonis, Juan Gelman.....

Monday afternoon
When I first read some poems by Nazim Hikmet I was in my late teens. They were published in an obscure international literary review in London, under the aegis of the British Communist Party. I was a regular reader. The Party line on poetry was crap, but the poems and stories published were often inspiring.

By that time Meyerhold had already been executed in Moscow. If I think particularly now of Meyerhold, it is because Hikmet admired him, and was much influenced by him when he first visited Moscow in the early '20s.

"I owe very much to the theatre of Meyerhold. In 1925 I was back in Turkey and I organised the first worker's Theatre in one of the industrial districts of Istanbul. Working in this theatre as director and writer, I felt that it was Meyerhold who had opened to us new possibilities of working for and with the audience."

After 1937, those new possibilities had cost Meyerhold his life, but in London readers of the Review did not yet know this. What struck me about Hikmet's poems when I first discovered them was their space; they contained more space than any poetry I had until then read. They didn't describe space; they came through it, they crossed mountains. They were also about action. They related doubts, solitude, bereavement, sadness, but these feelings followed actions rather than being a substitute for action. Space and actions go together. Their antithesis is prison, and it was in Turkish prisons that Hikmet, as a political prisoner, wrote half his life's work.

Wednesday

Nazim, I want to describe to you the table on which I'm writing. A white metal garden table, such as one might come across today in the grounds of a yali on the Bosphoros. This one is on the covered verandah of a small house in a southeast Paris suburb. This house was built in 1938, one of many houses built here at that time for artisans, tradesmen, skilled workers. In 1938 you were in prison. A watch was hanging on a nail above your bed. In the ward above yours three bandits in chains were awaiting their death sentence.

There are always too many papers on this table. Each morning the first thing I do, whilst sipping coffee, is to try to put them back into order. To the right of me there is a plant in a pot which I know you would like. It has very dark leaves. Their undersurface is the colour of damsons; on top the light has stained them dark brown. The leaves are grouped in threes, as if they were night butterflies - and they are the same size as butterflies - feeding from the same flower. The plant's own flowers are very small, pink and as innocent as the voices of kids learning a song in a Primary School. It's a kind of giant clover. This particular one came from Poland where the plant's name is Koniczyna. It was given to me by the mother of a friend who grew it in her garden near the Ukrainian border. She has striking blue eyes and can't stop touching her plants as she walks through the garden or moves around her house, just as some grandmothers can't stop touching their young grandchildren's heads.

> *"My love my rose,*
> *my journey across the Polish plain has begun:*
> *I'm a small boy happy and amazed*
> *a small boy*
> *looking at his first picture book*

> *of people*
> > *animals*
> > > *object, plants."*

In story-telling everything depends upon what follows what. And the truest order is seldom obvious. Trial and error. Often many times. This is why a pair of scissors and a reel of Scotch tape are also on the table. The tape is not fitted into one of those gadgets which makes it easy to tear off a length. I have to cut the tape with the scissors. What is hard is finding where the tape ends on the roll, and then unrolling it. I search impatiently, irritably with my finger nails. Consequently, when once I do find the end, I stick it on to the edge of the table, and I let the tape unroll until it touches the floor, then I leave it hanging there.

At times I walk out of the verandah into the adjoining room where I chat or eat or read a newspaper. A few days ago, I was sitting in this room and something caught my eye because it was moving. A minute cascade of twinkling water was falling, rippling, towards the verandah floor near the legs of my empty chair in front of the table. Streams in the Alps begin with no more than a trickle like this.

A reel of scotch tape stirred by a draught from a window is sometimes enough to move mountains.

Thursday evening

Ten years ago I was standing in front of a building in Istanbul near the Haydar-Pacha Station, where suspects were interrogated by the police. Political prisoners were held and cross-examined, sometimes for weeks, on the top floor. Hikmet was cross-examined there in 1938.

The building was not planned as a jail but as a massive administrative fortress. It appears indestructible and is built of bricks and silence. Prisons, constructed as such, have a sinister, but often, also, a nervous, make-shift air about them. For

69

It was Juan Muñoz whom I was waiting for in the Hotel Ritz in Madrid, and he was late because, as I explained, when he was working hard at night he was like a mechanic under a car, and he forgot about time.

example, the prison in Bursa where Hikmet spent ten years, was nick-named "the stone aeroplane", because of its irregular lay-out. The staid fortress I was looking at by the station in Istanbul had by contrast the confidence and tranquility of a monument to silence.

Whoever is inside here and whatever happens inside here - the building announced in measured tones - will be forgotten, removed from the record, buried in a crevice between Europe and Asia.

It was then that I understood something about his poetry's unique and inevitable strategy: it had to continually overreach its own confinement! Prisoners everywhere have always dreamt of the Great Escape, but Hikmet's poetry did not. His poetry, before it began, placed the prison as a small dot on the map of the world.

> "The most beautiful sea
>   hasn't been crossed yet.
> The most beautiful child
>   hasn't grown up yet.
> Our most beautiful days
>   we haven't seen yet.
> And the most beautiful words I wanted to tell you
>   I haven't said yet.
>
> They've taken us prisoner,
> they've locked us up:
>   me inside the walls,
>   you outside.
> But that's nothing.
> The worst
> is when people - knowingly or not -
> carry prison inside themselves...
> Most people have been forced to do this,
>
> honest, hard-working, good people
> who deserve to be loved as much as I love you."

His poetry, like a geometry compass, traced circles, sometimes intimate, sometimes wide and global, with only its sharp point inserted in the prison cell.

Friday morning

It was Juan Muñoz whom I was waiting for in the Hotel Ritz in Madrid, and he was late because, as I explained, when he was working hard at night he was like a mechanic under a car, and he forgot about time. After the Ritz incident he sent me a fax, which I'll quote. I'm not sure why. Maybe the why isn't my business. I'm simply acting as a postman between two dead men.

"I would like to introduce myself to you - I am a Spanish mechanic (cars only, not motorcycles) who spends most of his time lying on his back underneath an engine looking for it! But - and this is the important issue - I make the occasional art work. Not that I am an artist. No. But I would like to stop this nonsense of crawling in and under greasy cars, and become the Keith Richard of the art world. And if this is not possible to work like the priests, half an hour only, and with wine.

"I'm writing to you because two friends (one in Porto and one in Rotterdam) want to invite you and me to the basement of the Boyman's Car Museum and to other cellars (hopefully more alcoholic) in the old town of Porto.

"They also mentioned something about landscape which I did not understand. Landscape! I think maybe, it was something about driving and looking around, or looking around whilst driving around…

"Sorry Sir, another client just came in. Whoa! A Triumph Spitfire!"

I hear his laughter, echoing in the studio where he is alone with his silent figures.

Friday evening

Sometimes it seems to me that many of the greatest poems of the twentieth century - written by women as well as men - may be the most fraternal ever written. If so this has nothing to do with political slogans. It applies to Rilke who was apolitical, to Borges who was a reactionary, and to Hikmet who was a life-long communist. Our century was one of unprecedented massacres, yet the future it imagined (and sometimes fought for) proposed fraternity. Very few earlier centuries made such a proposal.

> *These men, Dino,*
> *who hold tattered shreds of light*
> *where are they going*
> *in this gloom, Dino?*
> *You, me too:*
> *we are with them, Dino.*
> *We too Dino*
> *have glimpsed the blue sky.*

Saturday

Maybe, Nazim, I'm not seeing you this time either. Yet I would swear to it that I am. You are sitting across the table from me on the verandah. Have you ever noticed how the shape of a head often suggests the mode of thinking which habitually goes on inside it? There are heads which relentlessly indicate speed of calculation. Others which reveal the determined pursuit of old ideas. Many these days betray the incomprehension of continuous loss. Your head - its size and your screwed up blue eyes - suggest to me the coexistence of many worlds with different skies, one within another, inside it; not intimidating, calm, but used to overcrowding.

I want to ask you about the period we're living today. Much of what you believed was happening in history, or believed should happen, has turned out to be illusory. Socialism, as you imagined it, is being built nowhere. Corporate capitalism advances unimpeded - although increasingly contested and the twin World Trade Towers have been blown up. The overcrowded world grows poorer every year. Where is the blue sky today that you saw with Dino?

Yes, those hopes, you reply, are in tatters, yet what does this really change? Justice is still a one-word prayer, as Ziggy Marley sings in your time now. The whole of history is about hopes being sustained, lost, renewed. And with new hopes come new theories. But for the overcrowded, for those who have little or nothing except, sometimes courage and love, hope works differently. Hope is then something to bite on, to put between the teeth. Don't forget this. Be realist. With hope between the teeth, comes the strength to carry on even when fatigue never lets up, comes the strength, when necessary, to choose not to shout at the wrong moment, comes the strength above all not to howl. A person, with hope between her or his teeth, is a brother or sister who commands respect. Those without hope in the real world are condemned to be alone. The best they can offer is only pity. And whether these hopes between the teeth are fresh or tattered makes little difference when it comes to surviving the nights and imagining a new day. Do you have any coffee?

I'll make some.

I leave the verandah. When I come back from the kitchen with two cups - and the coffee is Turkish - you have left. On the table, very near where the scotch tape is stuck, there is a book, open at a poem you wrote in 1962.

If I was a plane tree - I would rest in its shade
if I was a book
I would read, without being bored, on sleepless night
> *pencil I would not want to be, even between my own fingers*
if I was door
> *I would open for the good and shut for the wicked*
if I was window, a wide open window, without curtains
I would bring the city into my room
if I was a word
> *I would call out for the beautiful, the just, the true*
if I was word
> *I would softly tell my love.*

INTRODUCTION
& LITERATURE
FILM &
TELEVISION
VISUAL ART
PERFORMANCE

In a sense, all of John Berger's work can be considered within two frames; that of performance and conversation. That the two are linked is clear, but much performance is a monologue, and the essential element here is exchange. As Geoff Dyer observed in his preface, hierarchies are a closed circuit. They lead nowhere but towards their own reinforcement. So a performance that matters is one that opens itself, offers itself as a question, a consideration to be shared.

If John is a performer, it is primarily because he is a story teller. If the moment demanded that a single label be attached, it is perhaps this that he would choose. And the stories he tells are as much about the journey of ideas across centuries as they are about the passage of two people across a continent, or the tracing of a hairline by a hand before sleep. The story is a path by which we can join the ceaseless cycle of being. It is the track that remembering takes to walk into the future. The story that fully realises itself is always performed because, regardless of the teller's presence or absence, it is told with the whole body.

If the body then is offered, much as a stake, in the process, it would follow that the story matters. It is written on skin, in blood contained or shed, and it is never diluted by tears, but rather it becomes more concentrated. The story is one of justice and its shadow, of struggle and its tread, of motion then of rest, of place and its crop, its harvest of event.

It is the fable of ourselves and the other we have lost.

Now, the house is still. The evening presses its brow against the pane. Upstairs, in a warmer darkness, the child sleeps on into his own story, like a passing between lips and the shell of an ear in the game of whispers where, come the close, the story is both utterly changed and somehow still itself.

The story is a line cast into night; it is the ancient light that makes it through. It is a torch. It is bread and salt, and a gaze and a hearth.

It is what the hand is holding. It is the hand.

Vanishing Points
from a dialogue-in-progress

by Anne Michaels and John Berger

It was a long abandoned station on the Algoma line and to reach it we had to walk through the bush. Emerging from the wall of biting insects to the clearing made by the tracks. The long silent fraternity of those parallel lines. Immediately one sees railway tracks, one hears the noise of the train in one's mind. And then, only after, the silence.

Here, all the landscape, even the thick forest, seems dominated by the great Lake Superior. Miraculous immense Superior, "largest freshwater lake in the world."

I disappeared for hours, walking and looking on a deserted stretch of beach one can only reach by scrambling through bush over the shore cliffs. Here the beach grass was the most beautiful green I have ever seen, a colour my mind's eye has not forgotten over thirty years. Even in full sun, it was always cold. The persistent strong wind that has travelled over hundreds of miles of water. At ten I was an old hand at the task of looking to remember. That is certainly how I thought of it even then - looking in order to remember.

Once, my father made the climb, looking for me, exasperated with waiting for me to return to the camp site. Until he saw me - and then he said nothing except that they had been waiting because they wanted to walk to Frater. One of my brothers saw it on the map. The tiny italics, the hair with the tiny stitches on the map that indicate rail tracks. And when we emerged that day from the forest there it was, a wooden milepost, with a simple word, Frater, to indicate the station, the tracks, that silence. Without the human markings, one would never have thought what my father spoke aloud: the loneliest place on earth. Even then I knew it was not the loneliest place on earth, although I also knew that it was.

Meanwhile, as we walked home broken and grateful, the trains passed on and arrived at Union Station. All the sleepy children who woke disoriented in the bright lights of the platform. All the travellers who were greeted. All those with no one waiting.

The whistle, the incomparable sound of the railcars beginning to move, their great weight waking.

Happiness is no longer familiar to me, no longer familiar in my body. And because of this, I no longer know how to

remember Frater - because I know my memory of Frater is somehow now more true than my experience of it. And my memory of Frater, of standing in that immense silence where the station once was - always the station was simply that signpost - is also the memory contained in a photograph my father took there, the photograph of the wooden signpost, the tracks, the thick cold overcast sky. His wife, his three sons and his daughter are not in the photograph, but also somehow they are in the photograph.

The camera and the train. Both of them being means of transport - developed at more or less the same time. The shutter, the tunnels, the glass-roofed station, the plate, the rails, the lens, the switch points....

Later we ate thick sweet tomatoes with salt and fresh bread on the windy beach, holding on to our supper because otherwise the wind would seize it. I still taste my father's intense pleasure at that meal of tomatoes and bread, each element separate and together, the salt in the sweet juice, the lake, the wind. It seems to me now that every meal I've eaten since, is that meal. *Anne Michaels*

*

It was called the Broad Street line. A little suburban electric train running from the City of London to Kew Gardens. Many flower lovers and gardeners took the train to visit and marvel at the flowers in the botanical gardens, founded in the nineteenth century for the study of all the exotic plants being found in the far flung British Empire. In the early 1950's I took this train several times a week to go to a college in Richmond where I was a part-time teacher of painting. At one point the Broad Street line skirts the immense mainline marshalling yards of Willesden. It was here that all the traffic to and from Scotland the North-west was sorted, assembled and prepared. Rolling stock for passengers, first and second class, for goods, merchandise, coal, plying between Leighton Buzzard, Crewe, Preston, Carlisle, Glasgow and London. On each journey in the little train I awaited the moment when we approached and stopped at the Junction and I could look down on the yards. I

Psalm 139

JB. Dec 91

I will praise thee
for I am fearfully
and wonderfully made;
marvellous are thy works
and that my soul knoweth right well
My substance was not hid from thee
when I was made in secret
and curiously wrought
in the lowest parts
of the earth

Thine eyes did see my substance
yet being imperfect
and in thy book
all my members were written
which in continuance were fashioned
when as yet there was none of them

would sit glued to the window. I have heard people say that they first felt small when they gazed through a telescope at the night sky. For me it happened when I looked across Willesden Junction. In the early morning, at twilight, through rain, in the dark, under snow, in the summer heat, and day after ordinary day. Five years previously the railways in Britain had been nationalised. The London Midland and Scottish Railway which had owned these yards and overseen their continuous, haphazard, chaotic expansion, was now part of British Rail, which was said to belong to the people. As a consequence of nationalisation, the new coal freight trucks had double the capacity of the old ones. In the post-war dereliction there was somewhere a grandeur.

One morning I took the little train and got down at Willesden. I discovered Atlas Road, Common Lane and the North Pole Depot. And I began to draw the marshalling yards. I drew them again and again - as one might draw evening after evening the same woman, head inclined, sewing under the same lamp. Sometimes I drew them as if they were Bethsheba. Sometimes as if they were a Descent from the Cross. I exaggerate? Yes and No. It was a place of exaggeration. Coupling one truck to another and another. Making one train out of the wagons of two. Uncoupling a long train into fifty separate freight cars. Work of precision and exaggeration by day and night, under the arc lights and in daylight. Precision and Exaggeration.

From the drawings I wanted to make etchings. I remember printing some with Pru, and once or twice she came with me to Willesden. We walked along the Hythe Road and somehow got down on to an almost deserted stretch of the Permanent Way. To draw lines on copper into which acid ate had something in common with the rails. Pru spotted and picked up a pair of canvas gloves which had been dropped by a platelayer. She tried them on, laughing. They were huge and her wrists like her legs were very thin. She was the best painter of her generation. She might have been a Soviet constructivist. She died in the 1990s. Now she's helping me to remember as once, my cheek on her shoulder, my nose in her armpit, she helped me forget. *John Berger*

Into Arrival

by Anne Michaels

It will be in a station
with a glass roof
grimy with the soot
of every train and
they will embrace for every mile
of arrival. They will not
let go, not all the long way,
his arm in the curve
of her longing. Walking in a city
neither knows too well,
watching women with satchels
give coins to a priest for the war veterans;
finding the keyhole view of the church
from an old wall across the city, the dome
filling the keyhole precisely,
like an eye. In the home
of winter, under an earth
of blankets, he warms her skin
as she climbs in from the air.

There is a way our bodies
are not our own, and when he finds her
there is room at last
for everyone they love,
the place he finds,
she finds, each word of skin
a decision.

There is earth
that never leaves your hands,
rain that never leaves
your bones. Words so old they are broken
from us, because they can only be
broken. They will not
let go, because some love
is broken from love,
like stones
from stone,
rain from rain,
like the sea
from the sea.

We Are Both Story Tellers

by Simon McBurney

John Berger writes books. I stage events. Both of us address an audience. Or spectators. I am not sure how we work with each other. Most of the time I do not know how to describe how you work with anyone. There is always a gulf. How can I express what I imagine to another. How does one private and solitary imagination be shared with another. How can they be 'put together'? Surely they must do their own separate thing. Where to begin? There are the facts. A project to be completed. A show to put on. And then? Sometimes there are merely a few people. A man locked in the ice. A man who has lost his love. And lost his identity. Bodies to be held together by words and events that have yet to be imagined. And other times whole stories in books to be broken down to fragments to tell in another time and another place. Or sometimes a place to be inhabited both by words and bodies. The wedge between King's Cross and St Pancras for example. When I think about working with John I remember an opening passage in *And Our Faces, My Heart, Brief as Photos.*

We are both story tellers you and I. Lying on our backs we look up at the night sky.

John's kitchen is the warmest I know. The stove is upright and in the winter needs to be fed each morning. It is hot enough to keep a pot of soup ready to scald your throat. The table where we eat, where we talk is adjacent. If you sit with your back to the stove then you can feel the heat. If it is winter.

If summer then with your back to the stove the light will silhouette you from the one window from which you can see the apple trees in the garden, but which carry on into the Bertrand's field beyond, where the cows are out to pasture. If it is summer.

John usually sits there. When we are talking. I am not sure why. Nor would he be sure either. That is simply how I remember it as I am writing this now.

This is where stories began, under the aegis of that multitude of stars, which at night filch certitudes and sometimes return them as faith…

The ideas begin in that heat. Always beginning with questions.

'How shall we do it?'
'How many are we?'
'Five.'
'Then I would bring them to the boil and let them poach in the bouillon.'
'Good idea. Ferat have delicate flesh.'
'Ferat?'
'Lake fish. Like trout but a different species only found in the Lake of Geneva, the Lac Leman.'

Those who invented and first named the constellations were storytellers. Tracing an imaginary line between a cluster of stars gave them an image and an identity.

My father was an archaeologist. Which also means, though perhaps he would not like me to say this, being a story teller.

At work, holding flints in his hand like a good fishmonger holds a fillet out for your approval, he told me how the flint tools were made beside a fire.

'How do you know?'
'The loess is black from the cinders. The flints lay beside them in the earth for thousands of years.'
'Loess?'
'The soil we dug them out of. Dust blown off the glaciers over a hundred thousand years ago which covered everything.'
Human beings, he said, and wild dogs are the only species sharing food with others who are not part of their immediate

family. In the human animal this trait lead directly to the development of language.

The stars threaded on a line were like events threaded on a narrative.

And I have always imagined this to be true. The light. The food. The sharing in the darkness that makes sense of the darkness. Always leading to one conclusion. That when the story emerges the image and identity give a confirmation. Of something we need to be reminded of. Perhaps now more than ever. What is confirmed when we listen to a story together, when we watch a story together (Not you and I but us all, that is to say the number of people who make a human community, which is the number of people you find in a theatre), is that we not only listen to or look at the same thing at the same time, but we imagine the same thing at the same time… together. What we are often encouraged to think of as a 'private' or 'individual' event in the obscurity of our own unconscious is a shared and collective activity making sense of the darkness we all stand before.

Imagining the constellations did not of course change the stars, nor did it change the black emptiness that surrounds them. What it changed was the way people read the night sky.

THE THREE LIVES OF LUCIE CABROL

Directed by Simon McBurney. Based on a story by John Berger. Adapted by Simon McBurney & Mark Wheatley. Devised & Performed by Lilo Baur, Mick Barnfather, Hannes Flaschberger, Simon McBurney, Tim McMullan, Stefan Metz, Helene Patarot

Design: Tim Hatley; Lighting: Paule Constable; Sound: Christopher Shutt

'The famous Complicite technique is put to the service of a story, written by John Berger in 1979, about survival, love and justice. The eponymous heroine is a dwarfish Haute Savoie peasant, as old as the century, who is in turn a despised farm worker, fortune amassing market trader cruelly exiled from the village by her brothers and, finally, irrepressible ghost still nursing a passion for the globe-trotting Jean whom she once seduced in a cow shed. In Simon McBurney's exhilarating production the story becomes an unsentimental evocation of peasant life, a hymn to the tenacity of love and a Brechtian fable about the world's unfairness. In the extraordinary final transfiguration, the question of when justice will be done is answered by "When the living know what the dead have suffered." But the key point is that Complicite's brilliant technique is used to express Berger's ideas: Tim Hatley's earthen setting, the ensemble rhythms enshrining first rate performances from Lilo Baur as this Haute Savoie Mother Courage and McBurney himself as the earth spanning Jean and the imaginative use of planks, staves, boots and buckets are all determined by the story. Complicite have matured into greatness.' *Michael Billington, Guardian, March 1994*

Excerpt from *The Three Lives of Lucie Cabrol*

… She removed the lid of her milk can. She picked it up and, as you throw water out of a bucket, she hurled litres of milk into Henri's face. Whilst the milk was dripping from his hair, she screamed:

If you weren't a weasel I'd kill you!

The cheesemaker, swearing, tried to hit her, but she escaped, ran round the cauldron and vanished out of the door.

The story soon reached the ears of Marius à Brine. He found his daughter by the washing trough and he started to beat her, shouting:

Milk is not water! Milk is not water!

After a few blows he stopped. She was staring at him with her bright blue eyes. She had eyes the colour of forget-me-nots. Her look forced him to gather her into his arms and to press her face against his stomach.

Ah! My Cocadrille. You came out like that, didn't you? You can't help it. You just came out like that.

She stepped with her small feet onto his boots and then he carried her on his feet across the yard, repeating and laughing: The Cocadille! The Cocadrille!

And so the name Cocadrille, born of both hate and love, replaced the name Lucie. *Pig Earth, p110*

THE VERTICAL LINE

Directed by Simon McBurney. Written by John Berger with Sandra Voe

An INNERCITY production commissioned by Artangel
Produced in association with Complicite

*Jean-Marie Chauvet on discovering the cave in the Ardèche,
December 1994 …* 'Our light flashed onto a mammoth, then a
bear, then a lion with a semi-circle of little dots which seemed to
emerge from its muzzle like drops of blood, rhinoceroses... We
saw human hands, both positive and negative impressions. And
a frieze of other animals 30 feet long. Everything was so
beautiful, so fresh, almost too much so. Time was abolished, as
if the tens of thousands of years of separation no longer existed.
We were not alone, the painters were here too. We thought we
could feel their presence. We were disturbing them...'

'Over four nights in February 1999, the writer and art historian
John Berger, director Simon McBurney and the actress Sandra
Voe conducted an intimate 30,000 year-old journey, inscribing a
downward line through time 30 metres below central London.

Part theatrical event, part archaeological dig, *The Vertical
Line* was an oratorio of faces, voices, darkness and light; a one-
off excavation for small groups down 122 spiral steps into the
bowels of the disused Strand tube station, where a sequence of
audio-visual installations culminated in a live performance.

(Of) the Strand Station's two platforms… one closed in
1907, the other in 1994: on the same date, we later discovered,
as three French speologists led by Jean-Marie Chauvet first
opened up the cave in the Ardèche gorge.

We moved through these abandoned zones by instinct…
Half way down and we're in Corsica… It's 30,000 BC. Finally…
Pitch black and utter silence. Then the sound of footsteps
from the other end. "Can you hear me in the darkness?" and
those same voices - John's, Simon's and Sandra's - breathing by
our shoulders, whispering in our ears: yet still unseen…
Slowly, surely, we begin to see the cave-bear, the haematite, the
ochres and the browns through that deep, forgotten darkness
at the end of the Vertical Line far below London.'
Michael Morris, Co-Director, Artangel

TO THE WEDDING

*Directed by Simon McBurney. Based on the novel by John Berger.
Adapted by Simon McBurney, John Berger and Mark Wheatley*

A co-production with Penumbra Productions for BBC Radio 3.
Producer: Roger Elsgood; Sound: John Hunt
Cast: Annabel Arden, Mick Barnfather, Lilo Baur, Katrin Cartlidge,
Hannes Flaschberger, Susan Henry, Richard Hope, Kathryn Hunter,
Sandro Mabellini, Marcello Magni, Simon McBurney, Tim McMullan,
Aoife and Hélène Patarôt, Nicholas Robinson, Matthew Scurfield,
Lauren and Mathew Tata, Velibor Topic

'*To The Wedding* eschewed social realism and propagandism,
yet powerfully directed our imagination to the worst aspects of
Aids, apart from its ability to cause death - its effects on living.
As Ninon puts it with devastating clarity, "the gift of giving
myself has been taken away; if I give myself, I give death". But
if the play uncompromisingly faced the ghastliness of Aids, it
soared rather than depressed, and its broader subject matter
was not Aids at all. Zdena reveals her daughter's condition to
Thomas, the man sitting next to her on the coach (although
she hasn't been able to tell her friends - the piece was
excellent on the potency of fleeting encounters). With
Bergeresque wisdom, Thomas suggests that what has been lost
in the modern world is a sense of the precariousness of life.

The notion that life's risks can be controlled away leaves us
more vulnerable to them: we need fear to survive. And indeed
the pleasures of the eventual wedding - an exuberantly
sensuous, typically Italian village affair - are intensified by the
inescapable knowledge of how finite they must be, reinforced
by the device of intercutting Ninon's dying and wedding.
Berger's illuminations were wonderfully matched by Simon
McBurney's production, which unflashily rethought the
components of radio drama.'
Ann Karpf, Guardian, December 1997

Dramatic Collaborations
Goya's Last Portrait

by Nella Bielski and John Berger

A dramatic portrait of the artist, drawn from episodes of his life and the iconography of his art, and accompanied by reproductions of his etchings and drawings.

Goya There's not the slightest cause for alarm. I've already offered my services to the victors. Conquerors need painters and sculptors. Never forget that. Victory is ephemeral - as ephemeral as played music. Victory pictures are like wedding pictures, except there's no bride present. The bride is their own triumph. I don't know why, but it has always been so throughout history. So they want mother-fucking portraits of themselves with their invisible bride. And I can do these portraits like no one else can. I have a weakness for victors - above all for their collars, their boots, their victory robes. I think we were all meant to be triumphant. Before there was any destiny, we were children of a triumph. We were all born of an ejaculation.

Enter Doctor.

Doctor Your wife is asking to see you. I have one thing more to say to my husband, she says.

Exit Doctor hurriedly.

Goya Soon I'll do the Duke of Wellington. He insists upon a horse.

Gardener Don Federico has already gone into hiding.

Goya When the Whore's Desired One returns to sit on our throne, I shall paint him with a sword under his hand and a cocked hat under his arm. And if he won't sit for me, I'll paint him from memory. Looks in mirror. Everyone will forgive me.

Gardener The washerwomen say you're not so deaf you don't hear the clink of reales in the money bags. That's how you know when to change sides, they say.

Goya Everyone will forgive me.

Enter Doctor.

Doctor I regret to have to tell you, Don Francisco, it's too late. Your wife is dead.

Goya falls to his knees.

Goya Even my wife will forgive me. He remains kneeling with bowed head. Imperceptible sound of the sea. Abruptly he scrambles to his feet. If only men didn't forgive! He grasps the clothes line with both hands and walks beside it, holding it like a man in a gale. Do you know how much is unforgivable? Do you know there are acts which can never be forgiven? Nobody sees them. Not even God. Sea becomes louder. The perpetrators bury what they do from themselves and others with words. They call their victims names, they fasten labels to them, they repeat stories. Everything is prepared by curses and insults and whispering and speeches and chatter. The Devil works with words. He has no need of anything else. He distributes words and with the innocent working of the tongue and the roof of the mouth and the vocal cords, people talk themselves into evil, and afterwards with the same words and the same wicked numbers they hide what they've done, so it's forgotten, and what is forgotten is forgiven. He comes to a print. What is engraved doesn't forgive. He falls to his knees. Do not forgive us, O Lord. Let us see the unforgivable so we may never forget it. He somehow gets to his feet, walks to exit where Doctor entered. Forgive me, Josefa, forgive me…

From *A Question of Geography* by John Berger and Nella Bielski

Set under Stalin in the summer of 1952, the play focuses on Daria ('Dacha') who, having survived ten years in the Gulag, now lives in enforced permanent exile in Magadan, where she has a relationship with a doctor who is also a prisoner. As the play opens, she is expecting a visit from her 16 year old son Sacha, whom she has not seen since he was 18 months old.

…A beam of light falls on the middle of the stage. The rest in darkness. From the back of the auditorium a man's voice mixes with the other sounds and quickly dominates them. It is Serioja's voice reading his letter.

Serioja Dacha, my little darling, how to find the words now? Can you imagine, out of the darkness, out of the darkness of so many years, I received a letter from Katya. Like one of those flashes of light in Plato's cave. I learned that you are alive, that Sacha is almost grown up. How can such miracles

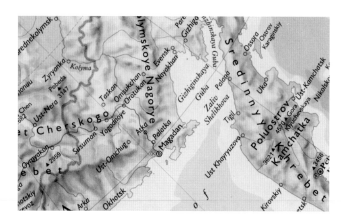

happen? I have to pinch myself to make sure I'm awake. Yes, I am. Fifteen years! For fifteen years, too, I haven't held a pen, so don't be hard on my handwriting. A guard fetched me this morning, brought me here to the office, gave me this pen and paper and said: You have the right of addressing one letter to your wife. And me, idiot that I am, I started to cry.

Where are you, my little one? I go back and back to the bridge in front of the Hermitage. Each paving stone, each arch of the bridge which we used to cross together, you in your black dress with a satchel - all, all is engraved. We were always in a hurry - for we had to go and fetch Sacha. I have lost my teeth and I have lost the toes of both feet. Since three years I have been on the stoves in the bath house, a merciful job for I'm no longer cold. I don't have much appetite, which is just as well. I suck with my gums and eating takes a long time. I'm not like an old man, I'm more like an old child who has forgotten his age. Hegel used to say that the difference between a dead person and a child is that the child doesn't have a memory. There our philosopher made a mistake because he couldn't foresee an intermediate category: one who is neither newborn, nor old, nor dead, nor living, yet who has a memory.

I always believed that the magic of your hands wasn't in your hands but was in the way your hands obeyed your eyes. You must have said I was dead and now I come back, alive! If I'm not transferred to the mines, I'll hold out, and you must go on thinking of me as dead, you will be closer, my heart, to the reality. My soul, my spirit, my memory have long since joined those of the dead who are, after all, the majority; and, in comparison with whom, the living are rare. Try not to think of me as being here, think of me rather as one who has already joined the Spirit of History which is watching over you from the furthest stars. I know every square millimetre of your body, astonishingly and eternally. My one wish is that Sacha may one day rejoin you. Fathers can be found anywhere. Know all this, my darling. As for me, I know it, and this knowledge is like a guiding star which will show me, until my last breath, where to place my frozen feet. We are already saved!

Everything on the stage resumes its normal appearance. Silence.

From *Isabelle: a Story in Shots* by John Berger and Nella Bielski

A prismatic imagination of the remarkable life of Isabelle Eberhardt, the young Swiss woman who crafted a new way of living and writing, disguised as a man, in North Africa at the beginning of the twentieth century.

Ship's deck. Isabelle descends a metal staircase to the crowded fourth-class deck, where the passengers, almost all of them North African, have improvised shelters against the wind and are sitting or sprawling on the deck. Many of the women are veiled. Some of the men are smoking narghiles. An unveiled woman, over fifty, wearing earrings and bracelets, holds out her hand as Isabelle passes. It could be the gesture of a beggar; Isabelle takes it as such and modestly looks for a coin. As she does so, she says in Arabic: 'Allahou Akbar!' The woman clasps Isabelle's hand to invite her to sit down beside her. Her name is Lella Hadra.

Lella Hadra Stay. What I have to tell you is for your two ears, not for the brass ear of money. In the poor mountains there lived a Bedouin shepherd girl called Smina. One day a French officer, a Roumi, asked her for water to give to his horse to drink. This Roumi officer fell in love with Smina - her eyes were like damsons. She said she could love him only if he became a Muslim... He took the oath and she named him Mabrouk. Smina's love for her Mabrouk was blind, yet she knew he would leave her. 'Next week I must go,' he said. 'I will come back soon.' And she replied: 'You want me no more, Mabrouk, you want to keep neither me nor your own word.'

Isabelle sips a glass of mint tea that has been offered to her.

Lella Hadra He left to become a major in his army, and he married a Roumia as all Roumis do.

Isabelle And Smina?

Lella Hadra She remained faithful to her love, she danced in cabarets, she became a camp-follower. She waits for her master to come back. ... When he comes back she will tell him he is a dog, a son of a bitch, who can love neither word nor woman, and as she says this her eyes - all wrinkled now - will...

Isabelle Will?

Lella Hadra ...will look upon the life they never lived.

Animals

by Despina Chronopoulos

"We patronize them for their incompleteness, for their tragic fate of having taken form so far below ourselves. And therein we err, and greatly err. For the animal shall not be measured by man. In a world older and more complete than ours they move finished and complete, gifted with extensions of the senses we have lost or never attained, living by voices we shall never hear. They are not brethren, they are not underlings; they are other nations caught with ourselves in the net of life and time, fellow prisoners of the splendour and travail of the earth."
H. Beston, 1971

Very rarely has man dared to venture into a non-human viewpoint taking reflection from there. For several decades, scientists have been testing animal intelligence through human-devised laboratory experiments, blinded by the most obvious anthropocentric biases, but yet smugly projecting their result to the rest of the species. Only because chimps resemble us the most, were they the most responsive to these tests. The introvert, non-spontaneous gorillas, who have developed completely different ways of social co-existence and expression, were much less responsive and therefore had been labelled for a long time as the dumbest ape.

Contact with them felt all the more rewarding to me because of this distance. You had to leave your own mode of expression behind – as much as you were able to - and step into that non human 'other space' in order to reach them and understand. The more distant the animal, the more fascinating the encounter, because the further you have to venture into the 'other' space.

In 1890, Darwin conducted his first mirror tests with apes.

"...in the zoological gardens I placed a looking glass in front of two orang utans, who had never before seen one. At first they gazed at their images in steady surprise, changing their point of view. Then they approached protruding their lips towards the images as if to kiss it, exactly as they had previously done towards each other. Next they made all sorts of grimaces, placed their hands behind it and looked behind it; finally they became frightened, looked increasingly cross and refused to look any longer."

Scientists have deduced from these and similar tests that apes

and other animals do not have self-recognition and therefore can have no self-awareness.

The people of the Biami tribe in Papua New Guinea have no access to slate or metallic surfaces and were assumed to ignore their own images. Edmund Carpenter, a visual anthropologist, describes their first reactions to mirrors. "They were paralysed after their first startled response – covering their mouths and ducking their heads. Some ran away, some

stood transfixed, staring at their images, only their stomach muscles betraying great tension… With recognition came fear. The individual would tremble uncontrollably, then turn away from the photograph."

Carpenter called this 'the terror of self awareness'. Of course, in this case nobody ventured the suggestion the Biami were lacking self consciousness before the scientists came along.

King

"Then I heard Vico's voice: We are being wiped off the earth, not the face of the earth, the face we lost long ago, the arse of the earth, il culo. We are their mistake, King, listen to me!... A mistake, King, is hated more than an enemy. Mistakes don't surrender as enemies do. There's no such thing as a defeated mistake. Mistakes either exist or they don't, and if they do, they have to be covered over. We are their mistake, King. Never forget that." From *King*

CARDBOARD CITIZENS is the UK's only homeless people's professional theatre company. The company produces theatre with, for and by homeless and ex-homeless people. We work with homeless and ex-homeless people, including asylum seekers and refugees, as creators, participants and audiences.

Cardboard Citizens was founded in 1991 and until 1995, when the company started to produce Forum Theatre work for schools, performances took place exclusively in homeless people's venues such as hostels and day centres. Our work in schools has become an important strand of our output and since 2000 has focussed as much on issues relating to refugees and asylum seekers, as to the more general concerns around homelessness.

Cardboard Citizens is the leading practitioner of Forum Theatre in the UK and offers training opportunities in Theatre of the Oppressed techniques developed by Augusto Boal. These are led by Boal himself and Adrian Jackson, Cardboard Citizens' Artistic Director and the English translator of Boal's books.

THE THEATRE OF THE OPPRESSED (TO) is the over-arching title given to the ensemble of techniques and approaches to theatre pioneered by the Brazilian theatre practitioner Augusto Boal. The common element of the various branches of this work is that all seek to make the power of theatre as a force for change available to everyone, particularly those in oppressed situations. The arenas of TO application range from the classroom to the council chamber, the union meeting to the therapeutic group, from the development charity to the homeless people's hostel.

Invisible Theatre is a form of guerrilla theatre or public provocation, designed to elicit discussion from an audience which does not know that it is witnessing theatre.

Forum Theatre is the best known and most widely practised form of Boal's useful theatre; it is an interactive form used particularly in situations where there is a shared oppression.

JOHN BERGER

Refusing to Accept the Absurdity of the World Picture Offered Us

by PLATFORM

PLATFORM came into existence in 1984 - at the high water mark of Thatcherism. In the years that followed, especially the critical early years when we were keenly aware of our fragility, John's writing acted as a lifeboat for us. But more than that, because not only was it a refuge from a storm of selfishness but also an absolute inspiration that another world was possible. As we lived and worked in the roar of London the voices of Marcel and Catherine and Martine in *Pig Earth* carried to us from the mountains of Haute Savoie. We picked over every detail of the Historical Afterword, argued about it, as if John was in the room with us. The ideas about cyclical time, (in contradistinction to the linearity, the obsession with 'progress' that had blinded the last century) - these ideas contributed directly to our thinking about working over the long-term, about our work needing to be for the dead and the unborn as well as the living.

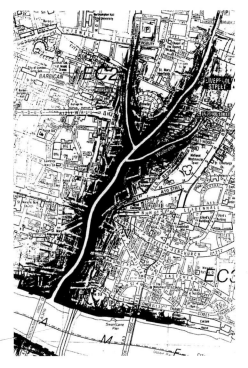

In *Refusing to Accept the Absurdity of the World Picture Offered Us*, PLATFORM will create a critical dialogue – no, more a conversation - with John. Using his texts as points of departure we will explore the nature of contemporary capitalism - specifically the transnational corporation - but in an intimate way, sometimes whispered, sometimes urgent. To deal with vastly powerful entities today, to confront systemic global dysfunction, perhaps requires an unprecedented calmness. A stillness. And a trusting of ourselves - the "intimate meditations about memory, alternatives, poetic flashes and evil… a voice which we've already heard somewhere inside our heads, and which, in our loneliness we've tended to dismiss." In a space in the heart of the City of London, using video, poetry, still images, the spoken word, we will look at these questions among others…

- *Why is there, in London, barely a trace of the most powerful corporation the world has ever seen?*
- *What are the fables of Gog & Magog?*
- *How is it possible to kill from a desk, from a computer terminal?*
- *How does consciousness begin to change?*

Since 1984 PLATFORM has established itself as one of Europe's leading exponents of social practice art, working on issues of social and ecological justice by combining the talents of artists, activists, researchers and educationalists. PLATFORM's projects have been recognised for their innovation and imagination both in Britain and internationally - over recent years it has been invited to make major presentations of its work in Bulgaria, Canada, Germany, Ireland, Spain, USA and Yugoslavia.

PLATFORM's current initiative 90% CRUDE (1996 - ongoing) is a ten-year, interdisciplinary enquiry into the culture and impact of transnational corporations, with particular reference to the oil industry. The performances, walks and publications include *Killing Us Softly* (now in production as a book, *The Desk Killer*, supported by the Lannan Foundation), *Loot! A Reckoning with the East India Company*, *The Museum of the Corporation* and *Unravelling the Carbon Web* - all have been acclaimed for raising critical questions regarding responsibility in the context of corporate impacts on human rights and climate change.

The work of PLATFORM has been featured in numerous books and articles (www.platformlondon.org). In 2000 PLATFORM received one of Britain's most prestigious environmental prizes, the Schumacher Award.

That Have Not Been Asked
Ten Dispatches about Endurance in Face of Walls

by John Berger

1

The wind got up in
the night and took our plans away.
(Chinese proverb)

2

The poor have no residence. They have homes because they remember mothers or grandfathers or an aunt who brought them up. A residence is a fortress, not a story; it keeps the wild at bay. A residence needs walls. Nearly everyone among the poor dreams of a small residence, like dreaming of rest. However great the congestion, the poor live in the open, where they improvise, not residences, but places for themselves. These places are as much protagonists as their occupants; the places have their own lives to live and do not, like residences, wait on others. The poor live with the wind, with dampness, flying dust, silence, unbearable noise (sometimes with both; yes, that's possible!) with ants, with large animals, with smells coming from the earth, rats, smoke, rain, vibrations from elsewhere, rumours, nightfall, and with each other. Between the inhabitants and these presences there are no clear marking lines. Inextricably confounded, they together make up the place's life.

"Twilight was setting in; the sky wrapped in cool grey fog, was already being closed off by darkness; and the wind, after spending the day rustling stubble and bare bushes that had gone dead in preparation for winter, now lay itself down in still low places on the earth...."

The poor are collectively unseizable. They are not only the majority on the planet, they are everywhere and the smallest event speaks of them. This is why the essential activity of the rich today is the building of walls - walls of concrete, of electronic surveillance, of missile barrages, minefields, frontier controls, and opaque media screens.

3

The lives of the poor are mostly grief, interrupted by moments of illumination. Each life has its own propensity for illumination and no two are the same. (Conformism is a habit cultivated by the well-off.) Illuminated moments arrive by way of tenderness and love - the consolation of being recognised and needed and embraced for being what one suddenly is! Other moments are illuminated by an intuition, despite everything, that the human species serves for something.

"Nazar tell me something or other - something more important than anything."

Aidym turned down the wick in the lamp in order to use less paraffin. She understood that, since there was something or other in life that was more important than anything, it was essential to take care of every good that there was.

"I don't know the thing that really matters, Aidym," said Chagataev. " I haven't thought about it, I've never had time. But if we've both of us been born, then there must be something in us that really matters."

Aidym agreed: "A little that does matter... and a lot that doesn't."

Aidym prepared supper. She took a flat bread out of a sack, spread it with sheep's fat and broke it in half. She gave Chagataev the big half, and took the small half herself. They silently chewed their food by the weak light of the lamp. In the Ust-Yurt and the desert it was quiet, uncertain and dark."

4

From time to time despair enters into the lives which are mostly grief. Despair is the emotion which follows a sense of betrayal. A hope against hope (which is still far from a promise) collapses or is collapsed; despair fills the space in the soul which was occupied by that hope. Despair has nothing to do with nihilism.

Nihilism, in its contemporary sense, is the refusal to believe in any scale of priorities beyond the pursuit of profit, considered as the end-all of social activity, so that, precisely: everything has its price. Nihilism is resignation before the contention that Price is all. It is the most current form of human cowardice. But not one to which the poor often succumb.

"He began to pity his body and his bones; his mother had once gathered them together for him from the poverty of her

flesh - not because of love and passion, not for pleasure, but out of the most everyday necessity. He felt as if he belonged to others, as if he were the last possession of those who have no possessions, about to be squandered to no purpose, and he was seized by the greatest, most vital fury of his life."

[A word of explanation about these quotations. They are from the stories of the great Russian writer, Andrei Platonov (1899-1951). He wrote about the poverty which occurred during the Civil War and later during the forced collectivisation of Soviet agriculture in the early 1930's. What made this poverty unlike more ancient poverties was the fact that its desolation contained shattered hopes. It fell to the ground exhausted, it got to its feet, it staggered, it marched on amongst shards of betrayed promises and smashed words. Platonov often used the term dushevny bednyak, which means literally poor souls. It referred to those from whom everything had been taken so that the emptiness within them was immense and in that immensity only their soul was left - that's to say their ability to feel and suffer. His stories do not add to the grief being lived, they save something. "Out of our ugliness will grow the world's heart." he wrote in the early 1920s.

The world today is suffering another form of modern poverty. No need to quote the figures; they are widely known and repeating them again only makes another wall of statistics.

More than half the world population live with less than $2 a day. Local cultures with their partial remedies - both physical and spiritual - for some of life's afflictions are being systematically destroyed or attacked. The new technology and means of communication, the free market economy, productive abundance, parliamentary democracy, are failing, so far as the poor are concerned, to keep any of their promises beyond that of the supply of certain cheap consumerist goods, which the poor can buy when they steal.

Platonov understood living modern poverty more deeply than any other storyteller I have come across.]

5

The secret of storytelling amongst the poor is the conviction that stories are told so that they may be listened to elsewhere, where somebody, or perhaps a legion of people, know better than the storyteller or the story's protagonists, what life means. The powerful can't tell stories: boasts are the opposite of stories, and any story however mild has to be fearless and the powerful today live nervously.

A story refers life to an alternative and more final judge who is far away. Maybe the judge is located in the future, or in the past that is still attentive, or maybe somewhere over the hill, where the day's luck has changed (the poor have to refer often to bad or good luck) so that the last have become first.

Story-time (the time within a story) is not linear. The living and the dead meet as listeners and judges within this time, and the greater the number of listeners felt to be there, the more intimate the story becomes to each listener. Stories are one way of sharing the belief that justice is imminent. And for such a belief, children, women and men will fight at a given moment with astounding ferocity. This is why tyrants fear storytelling: all stories somehow refer to the story of their fall.

"Wherever he went, he only had to promise to tell a story and people would take him in for the night: a story's stronger than a Tsar. There was just one thing: if he began telling stories before the evening meal, no-one ever felt hungry and he didn't get anything to eat. So the old soldier always asked for a bowl of soup first."

The worst cruelties of life are its killing injustices. Almost all promises are broken. The poor's acceptance of adversity is neither passive nor resigned. It's an acceptance which peers behind the adversity and discovers there something nameless.

6

The worst cruelties of life are its killing injustices. Almost all promises are broken. The poor's acceptance of adversity is neither passive nor resigned. It's an acceptance which peers behind the adversity and discovers there something nameless. Not a promise, for (almost) all promises are broken; rather something like a bracket, a parenthesis in the otherwise remorseless flow of history. And the sum total of these parentheses is eternity.

This can be put the other way round: on this earth there is no happiness without a longing for justice.

Happiness is not something to be pursued, it is something met, an encounter. Most encounters, however, have a sequel; this is their promise. The encounter with happiness has no sequel. All is there instantly. Happiness is what pierces grief.

'We thought there was nothing left in the world, that everything had disappeared long ago. And if we were the only ones left, what was the point of living?

'We went to check, said Allah. 'Were there any other people anywhere? We wanted to know.'

Chagataev understood them and asked if this meant they were now convinced about life and wouldn't be dying any more.

'Dying's no use,' said Cherkezov. 'To die once - now you might think that's something necessary and useful. But dying once doesn't help you to understand your own happiness - and no one gets the chance to die twice. So dying gets you nowhere.'"

7

"Whilst the rich drank tea and ate mutton, the poor were waiting for the warmth and for the plants to grow."

The difference between seasons, as also the difference between night and day, shine and rain, is vital. The flow of time is turbulent. The turbulence makes life-times shorter - both in fact and subjectively. Duration is brief. Nothing lasts. This is as much a prayer as a lament.

"(The mother) was grieving that she had died and forced her children to mourn for her; if she could have, she would have gone on living forever so that nobody should suffer on her account, or waste, on her account, the heart and the body to which she had given birth....but the mother had not been able to stand living for very long."

Death occurs when life has no scrap left to defend.

8

"....it was as if she were alone in the world, free from happiness and sorrow, and she wanted to dance a little, right away, to listen to music, to hold hands with other people...."

They are accustomed to living in close proximity with one another, and this creates its own spatial sense; space is not so

IN THE KINGDOM OF THE OLIVE TREES BY JEAN MOHR

much an emptiness as an exchange. When people are living on top of one another, any action taken by one has repercussions on the others. Immediate physical repercussions. Every child learns this.

There is a ceaseless spatial negotiation which may be considerate or cruel, conciliating or dominating, unthinking or calculated, but which recognises that an exchange is not something abstract but a physical accommodation. Their elaborate sign languages of gestures and hands are an expression of such physical sharing. Outside the walls collaboration is as natural as fighting; scams are current, and intrigue, which depends upon taking a distance, is rare. The word private has a totally different ring on the two sides of the wall. On one side it denotes property; on the other an acknowledgement of the temporary need of someone to be left, as if alone, for a while. Every site inside the walls is rentable - every square meter counted; every site outside risks to become a ruin - every sheltering corner counted.

The space of choices is also limited. They choose as much as the rich, perhaps more, for each choice is starker. There are no colour charts which offer a choice between one hundred and seventy different shades. The choice is close-up -between this or that. Often it is made vehemently, for it entails the refusal of what has not been chosen. Each choice is quite close to a sacrifice. And the sum of the choices is a person's destiny.

9

No development (the word has a capital D as an article of faith on the other side of the walls) no insurance. Neither an open future nor an assured future exist. The future is not awaited. Yet there is continuity; generation is linked to generation. Hence a respect for age since the old are a proof of this continuity - or even a demonstration that once, long ago, a future existed. Children are the future. The future is the ceaseless struggle to see that they have enough to eat and the sometimes-chance of their learning with education what the parents never learnt.

"When they finished talking, they threw their arms around each other. They wanted to be happy right away, now, sooner than their future and zealous work would bring results in personal and in general happiness. The heart brooks no delay, it sickens, as if believing in nothing."

Here the future's unique gift is desire. The future induces the spurt of desire towards itself. The young are more flagrantly young than on the other side of the wall. The gift appears as a gift of nature in all its urgency and supreme assurance. Religious and community laws still apply. Indeed amongst the chaos which is more apparent than real, these laws become real. Yet the silent desire for procreation is incontestable and overwhelming. It is the same desire that will forage for food for the children and then seek, sooner or later, (best sooner) the consolation of fucking again. This is the future's gift.

10

The multitudes have answers to questions which have not yet been posed, and they have the capacity to outlive the walls.

The questions are not yet asked because to do so requires words and concepts which ring true, and those currently being used to name events have been rendered meaningless: Democracy, Liberty, Productivity, etc.

With new concepts the questions will soon be posed, for history involves precisely such a process of questioning. Soon? Within a generation.

Meanwhile, the answers abound in the multitudes' multiple ingenuities for getting by, their refusal of frontiers, their search for holes in the walls, their adoration of children, their readiness when necessary to become martyrs, their belief in continuity, their recurring acknowledgement that life's gifts are small and priceless.

Trace with a finger tonight her (his) hairline before sleep.

Contributors

Asu Aksoy is a research associate at Goldsmiths College, University of London, undertaking research on Turkish on Turkish and Kurdish migrants in London.

Dr Jane Anderson is Consultant Physician at Homerton University NHS Foundation Trust.

Holly Aylett is a writer, lecturer and managing editor of the film magazine *Vertigo*.

Anthony Barnett is the Editor of openDemocracy.net. The author of *Iron Britannia*, *Soviet Freedom* and *This Time*, he was a Fellow of the TNI and the founding director of Charter 88.

Lilo Baur is an actor. She performed in Complicite's *The Three Lives of Lucie Cabrol*.

Katya Berger Andreadakis is a translator, journalist and cinema critic.

Yves Berger is an artist. He lives in France.

Nella Bielski is a novelist and playwright. Her most recent book, *The Year Is '42*, was published in 2004. She lives in Paris.

Gavin Bryars is an internationally acclaimed composer.

Nichola Bruce directed the award winning *I Could Read The Sky* and is currently a NESTA Fellow, investigating perception, memory and the moving image.

Tony Calland is a former partner of John Sassal, the subject of *A Fortunate Man*.

Paul Carlin is an award-winning documentary film-maker.

Gianni Celati is a writer and film-maker.

John Christie is an artist, designer, book- and film-maker. He has worked with John Berger on several singular book and television projects.

Jonathan Christie is an artist and graphic designer.

Despina Chronopoulos is a specialist in the protection of endangered species and the author of *Orphan Gorillas*.

Chris Darke is a freelance writer and critic, the author of *Light Readings* (Wallflower Press) and *Alphaville* (IB Tauris, 2005).

Mike Dibb is an award-winning documentary film-maker and has worked on numerous projects with John Berger. His most recent film is a portrait of musician Keith Jarrett.

Geoff Dyer is an acclaimed writer and critic. He is the author of many books, among them a study of John Berger's work.

Mehmet Emir is a photographer from Dersim in Turkey, living in Vienna, and curator of the exhibition *Mein Vater und Ich*.

Gareth Evans is a writer and film programmer. He works on the film pages of *Time Out London* and edits the film journal *Vertigo* (www.vertigomagazine.co.uk).

Moris Farhi is an author of Turkish origins living in London. He is the author of *Young Turk* among many other books.

Gene Feder is a GP in Hackney and Professor of primary care R&D at Queen Mary University.

Timothy O'Grady is the author, with photographer Steve Pyke, of *I Could Read the Sky*. His most recent novel is *Light*.

Maggi Hambling is an artist. There have been major exhibitions of her work at the National Gallery, National Portrait Gallery and the Serpentine Gallery. She won the Jerwood Prize for Painting in 1995.

Iona Heath is a GP in Kentish Town and author of *The Mystery of General Practice*.

Richard Hollis is a graphic designer and design historian. He has worked on several books with John Berger, among them *G.*, *Ways of Seeing* and *A Seventh Man*. He is the author of *Graphic Design: A Concise History*.

Patrick Hutt is a junior doctor and author of *Confronting an Ill Society*.

Adrian Jackson is artistic director of theatre company Cardboard Citizens, a teacher, translator and frequent collaborator with Augusto Boal. Their most recent project was *The Art of Legislation*.

Colin MacCabe is a writer, producer and distinguished Professor of English and Film at the University of Pittsburgh. His most recent book is *Godard: Portrait of the Artist at 70*.

Simon McBurney is an internationally acclaimed theatre-maker and actor. He is artistic director of Complicite.

Anne Michaels lives in Toronto. She is the author of the Orange Prize-winning novel *Fugitive Pieces* and three collections of poetry, *The Weight of Oranges*, *Miner's Pond* and *Skindivers*.

Jean Mohr is an internationally renowned photographer, who has worked with the UN and ICRC among many agencies. He has collaborated with John Berger on three highly influential books.

James Mollison is a photographer. He consults for Fabrica, contributes to *COLORS* and works for publications in Italy and the UK. He has published four books: *Lavoratori*, *O Bologna!*, *Kosovars* and *James and Other Apes*.

Timothy Neat is a writer, historian and film-maker. He has published a number of books of Scottish cultural history and is currently completing a biography of Hamish Henderson.

Emine Sevgi Ozdamar is a well-known German-Turkish novelist, winner of the Ingeborg Bachmann prize. *Mother Tongue* and *Life is a Caravanserai* are available in English.

Michael Ondaatje lives in Toronto. The author of many acclaimed books, he won the Booker Prize for *The English Patient*. His most recent novel is *Anil's Ghost*.

Nick Partridge is Chief executive of The Terrence Higgins Trust.

Platform (www.platformlondon.org) has been working on interdisciplinary projects dealing with cultural, social and ecological justice for more than 20 years. The collective is based near the Thames.

Sally Potter is a film-maker. Her films include *Orlando* and *The Tango Lesson*. Her most recent feature is *Yes*.

Chris Rawlence is a film-maker, writer and librettist. He has directed numerous tv programmes and series, specialising in neurological documentaries and operas. More recently he's been making movies within the palliative care community, developing a musical across three London hospices and setting up an Internet Channel for the life-threatened.

Kevin Robins is Professor of Sociology at City University, London, working on Turkish migration and European culture.

Di Robson is an independent cultural event producer, consultant and lecturer. She works across all art forms and has particular expertise in programme and festival creation and delivery

Michael Rosen is a poet, broadcaster and writer, whose books include *Carrying the Elephant*.

Sukhdev Sandhu is lead film critic for *The Daily Telegraph* and writes widely on cultural issues. He is the author of the acclaimed *London Calling: How Black and Asian Writers Imagined a City*.

Jane Simpson is a junior doctor.

Alain Tanner is a film director. He has made three features with John Berger.

Latife Tekin is one of Turkey's leading novelists. Her books *Berji Kristin: Tales from the Garbage Hills* and *Dear Shameless Death* are published in English.

Marc Trivier is a photographer. His books include *Photographies*, *Paradise Lost* and *My Beautiful*. He lives in Belgium.

Milena Trivier is studying film in Brussels.

Patrick Wright is one of Britain's most distinctive cultural critics and broadcasters. He has published a number of books on aspects of national memory, history and identity.

Dai Vaughan was formerly a documentary film editor and worked on several films with John Berger. He is also a writer. His most recent publications include *Totes Meer* and *Germs*.

Yuksel Yavuz is a filmmaker of Turkish background living in Germany. He is the director of *Mein Vater der Gastarbeiter* and *Kleine Freiheit*.

Gary Younge is a journalist writing for *The Guardian*.

Selected Bibliography

*The following contains only major publications by John Berger, and those books
and artefacts in which he has played a major collaborative part. It does not include
the numerous novels, collections and catalogues to which he has contributed a preface,
foreword, introduction or story. It also does not document the uncollected essays,
articles, stories, reviews and interviews that have not appeared in book form.
Note: the covers shown are from various editions. Not all titles are currently in print.
A number of the titles below have been made with others. See relevant articles.*

A Painter of Our Time

The Moment of Cubism

G.

And Our Faces, My Heart, Brief as Photos

I Send You This Cadmium Red

At the Edge of the World

Permanent Red

The Look of Things

About Looking

About Time

Pages of the Wound

Vertical Line

The Foot of Clive

Ways of Seeing

Pig Earth

The White Bird

Road Directions

Isabelle

Corker's Freedom

Another Way of Telling

Once in Europa

Keeping a Rendezvous

Photocopies

The Shape of a Pocket

A Fortunate Man

A Seventh Man

Lilac and Flag

A Question of Geography

To the Wedding

Titian: Nymph and Shepherd

Art and Revolution

The Success and Failure of Picasso

Jonah Who Will Be 25 in the Year 2000

Goya's Last Portrait

King

Here Is Where We Meet

John Berger: Here Is Where We Meet
A Season, London 11th April-18th May 2005

WWW.JOHNBERGER.ORG | 020 8510 9786

Live Events Calendar

What the Hand Is Holding: Writing Now
11 APRIL 7.30

Readings by and discussion with John Berger, Geoff Dyer, Anne Michaels, Timothy O'Grady and Michael Ondaatje. Chaired by Patrick Wright. See pages 16-23.
Queen Elizabeth Hall, South Bank Centre, SE1. 08703 800 400; www.rfh.org.uk

A Seventh Man: Migration and Photography
12 APRIL 6.30

First in a series of events considering the impact of the path-breaking book by John Berger and Jean Mohr. Panel discussion around migration and photography with Jean Mohr, photographer Mehmet Emir and writer Timothy O'Grady. Moderated by Asu Aksoy. See pages 52-53 and below.
Austrian Cultural Forum London 28 Rutland Gate, SW7. 020 7584 8653; www.austria.org.uk/culture

John Berger: a Telling Eye
13 APRIL 6.00

Panel discussion with Jean Mohr, John Christie and Maggi Hambling on collaborations between writers and artists. Moderated by Geoff Dyer. See exhibition below and pages 50-59 & 66.
Lyttelton Theatre, National Theatre, South Bank, SE1. 020 7452 3400; www.nationaltheatre.org.uk

John Berger: a Film and Television Retrospective
14-30 APRIL

A major presentation of John Berger's work with the moving image. See overleaf for full listings and also pages 24-43.
National Film Theatre, South Bank, SE1. 020 7928 3232; www.bfi.org.uk/nft

Vanishing Points (working title)
14-16 APRIL 7.00

Commissioned especially for this season, an exploration of railways, migration and memory, taking place in and around King's Cross Station. Written by John Berger and Anne Michaels. Directed by Simon McBurney. In association with Complicite. See pages 74-76.
German Gym Kings Cross/ St Pancras. Please phone 020 8510 9786 for further information or visit the website.

Yes
17 APRIL 6.00

Special preview screening of the new film Yes by Sally Potter, with the director in attendance.
See pages 32-34.
Ritzy Cinema, Brixton Oval, Coldharbour Lane, SW2 08707550062 www.picturehouses.co.uk

John Berger and Geoff Dyer in Conversation
19 APRIL 6.20

See overleaf for full details.
National Film Theatre, South Bank, SE1. 020 7928 3232; www.bfi.org.uk/nft

Titian: a Portrait
22 APRIL 7.00

In this reading and slide presentation, John Berger and his daughter Katya Berger explore the meaning of Titian in art and their own relationship. See page 63.
National Portrait Gallery, St Martin's Place, WC2. 020 7306 0055; www.npg.org.uk

Caught Between Culture and Commerce? Independent Film and Television in the UK and Beyond A Panel Discussion
26 APRIL 6.20

See overleaf for full details.
National Film Theatre, South Bank, SE1. 020 7928 3232; www.bfi.org.uk/nft

A Fortunate Man
26 APRIL 7.30

An exploration of the enduring importance of the book by John Berger and Jean Mohr about general practice and social medicine. Discussion with writers Michael Rosen and Sukhdev Sandhu and doctors Iona Heath, Patrick Hutt, Jane Simpson and Tony Calland. Includes a showing of the BBC documentary drawn from the book. Moderated by GP and Professor of Primary Care R&D at Queen Mary University, Gene Feder. See pages 50-51.
Drapers Lecture Theatre, Geography Building, Queen Mary University of London, Mile End Road, E1. 020 8510 9786.

A Small Freedom 'Kleine Freiheit'
27 APRIL 6.00

A Seventh Man event. Screening of Turkish/German feature A Small Freedom, directed by Yuksel Yavuz, about African and Kurdish teenagers in Hamburg. Plus a discussion with the director and commentator Sukhdev Sandhu. See pages 52-53 and below
Goethe Institute, 50 Princes Gate, Exhibition Road, SW7. 020 7596 4000; www.Goethe.de/london

To the Wedding
27 APRIL 7.00

A discussion, inspired by the novel by John Berger, about responses to HIV/AIDS, its social effects and the nature of stigma; with panellists to include Nick Partridge, Chief executive of The Terrence Higgins Trust and Dr Jane Anderson, Consultant Physician, Homerton University NHS Foundation Trust. See page 79.
The London Lighthouse, Lancaster Road, W11. 020 7792 1200; www.tht.org.uk

My Beautiful
6 MAY 6.30

Accompanying the exhibition of the same name, a reading around the work of Giacometti by John Berger, photographer Marc Trivier and artist Yves Berger.
See pages 60-62 and below
Purdy Hicks Gallery, 65 Hopton St, Bankside, SE1. 020 7401 9229.

Love is the Devil +
I Could Read the Sky
8 MAY

Special double bill of independent British films. *Love is the Devil*, John Maybury's imaginative biography of Francis Bacon, will be introduced by photographer Marc Trivier, who knew and photographed the artist. *I Could Read the Sky* is adapted from Timothy O'Grady's book and poetically explores the life and memory of an Irish migrant in London. It will be introduced by director Nichola Bruce.
See pages 22-23.
Curzon Soho Cinema, Shaftesbury Avenue, W1. 020 7734 2255; www.curzoncinemas.com

Goya's Last Portrait
9 MAY 6.30

A reading by John Berger and Nella Bielski from their drama on the life and work of the Spanish artist. Joining them will be actor Lilo Baur.
See page 80.
National Gallery, Trafalgar Square, WC2. 020 7747 2885; www.nationalgallery.org.uk

The Look Exchanged: Considering Animal Perception
10 MAY 7.00

John Berger and Despina Chronopoulos in conversation about the human response to the non-human, and vice-versa. With photographer James Mollison presenting images from his book of primate portraits James and Other Apes. See page 83.
ICA, The Mall, SW1. 020 7930 3647; www.ica.org.uk

King: A Street Story and Response
11-12 MAY 8.00

Performance and discussion reacting to the novel about homelessness by John Berger. Presented by Cardboard Citizens. See page 84.
In the East End. Please phone 020 8510 9786 for further information or visit the website.

And Our Faces, My Heart, Brief as Photos
12 MAY 7.00

Reading by John Berger to mark republication of his important and innovative book. See back cover.
London Review Bookshop, 14 Bury Place, Bloomsbury, WC1. 020 7269 9030; www.lrb.co.uk/lrbshop

Refusing to Accept the Absurdity of the World Picture Offered Us
13 MAY 7.30

Inspired by John Berger's writings, London-based group Platform will explore the nature of contemporary capitalism and the transnational corporation. See page 85.
A venue between Bank and Liverpool St. Phone 020 7403 3738; email info@platformlondon.org for further information.

A Seventh Man: Then and Now
17 MAY 6.00

A discussion inspired by John Berger and Jean Mohr's book about migrant workers. With writers Gary Younge, Letife Tekin, Moris Farhi, Emine Sevgi Ozdamar (tbc) and migrant cultures research associate Asu Aksoy. Moderated by Professor of Sociology, Kevin Robins.
See pages 52-53.
Institute of International Visual Arts 6-8 Standard Place, Rivington St, Shoreditch, EC2. 020 7729 9616; www.iniva.org

John Berger and Simon McBurney in Conversation
18 MAY 7.30

John Berger and internationally acclaimed actor / theatre director McBurney of Complicite consider the nature of creative collaborations. See pages 77-79.
Purcell Room, South Bank Centre, SE1. 08703 800 400; www.rfh.org.uk

Exhibitions

John Berger: a Telling Eye
Visual Collaborations with Jean Mohr, John Christie and Maggi Hambling.
5 APRIL-28 MAY MON-SAT: 10AM-11PM

Presentations of *A Seventh Man*, *I Send You This Cadmium Red*, *Pages of the Wound* and drawings by Maggi Hambling.
See pages 50-59 & 66.
Lyttelton Circle Foyer Gallery, National Theatre, South Bank, SE1. 020 7452 3400; www.nationaltheatre.org.uk

Mein Vater und Ich
12 APRIL-12 MAY MON-FRI: 9AM-5PM

Photographs documenting the life and experiences of a (Turkish) Kurdish guestworker in Vienna, also bringing out the relationship between a father and son. By Mehmet Emir.
Austrian Cultural Forum London, 28 Rutland Gate, SW7. 020 7584 8653; www.austria.org.uk/culture

John Berger: Portraits by Jean Mohr
14 APRIL-18 MAY
MON-FRI: 9.00AM-6.00

Photographs drawn from over four decades of friendship.
Foyer, Social Science Building, City University, St John St, EC4. 0208 510 9786

My Beautiful
5-21 MAY MON-FRI: 10.00AM-5.30; WED: TO 7.00; SAT: 11.00AM-5.00

An exhibition of photography, drawings and text exploring the work of Giacometti, by John Berger, photographer Marc Trivier and artist Yves Berger. See pages 60-62.
Purdy Hicks Gallery, 65 Hopton St, Bankside, SE1. 020 7401 9229.

Ways of Seeing Revisited
FROM 7 MAY DAILY: 10.00AM-5.50

An exhibition of archive material surrounding the hugely influential book and television series by John Berger and Mike Dibb, with regular screenings of the four part series. See pages 26-30.
Tate Britain, Millbank, SW1. 020 7887 8000; www.tate.org.uk

John Berger: Here Is Where We Meet
A Season, London 11th April-18th May 2005

NATIONAL FILM THEATRE

Film & Television Retrospective

Ways of Seeing Parts 1 & 2 + Drawn from Life

THU 14 APR 6.10 NFT2*

FRI 22 APR 6.00 NFT2

One of the most influential television series ever made, *Ways of Seeing* (BBC 1972/Dir Mike Dibb; 2x30 mins) revolutionised how art and advertising were perceived and read. Crafting a tapestry of ideas and images drawn widely from visual culture, Berger created a compelling argument about art's relation to power that has become a benchmark of interpretation. *Drawn from Life* (Granada 1962/Dir Mike Wooller) was among Berger's earliest television projects: a Manchester-made series which tested art against experience through conversations with 'ordinary people' about the relation of paintings to their lives. Years ahead of its time, it displays a remarkable empathy. We are screening two of the series' 28-minute episodes.

Total 116 mins.

*Introduction by Mike Dibb.

Ways of Seeing Parts 3 & 4 + 10,000 Days, 93,000 Hours, 33 Years of Effort + An Artist from Moscow

THU 14 APR 8.30 NFT2*

FRI 22 APR 8.20 NFT2

The concluding episodes (2x30 mins) in Berger's path-breaking and politically humane analysis of fine art and its commercial counterparts remain important – and relevant – viewing. As do two lyrical odes to idealism and resistance in art, made for landmark arts strand *Monitor* (BBC 1965 & 1969; 2x28 mins) and revealing Berger's desire never to separate a reading of culture

from the life and times that inspired it. The first is a rumination on French postman-turned-visionary builder Ferdinand Cheval, while the latter offers a committed portrait of Soviet sculptor Ernst Neizvestny.

Total 116 mins.

*Introduction by Mike Dibb.

Joint ticket available £10.50, concs £8.25.

The Salamander La Salamandre

Switzerland 1971/Dir Alain Tanner. With Bulle Ogier, Jean-Luc Bideau, Jacques Denis, Véronique Alain.

129 mins. J-Cert 15.

FRI 15 APR 5.45 NFT2

THU 21 APR 8.30 NFT2

The 1970s saw Berger make a decisive move to Europe and begin his extraordinarily fruitful collaboration with Swiss director Tanner. The first of three films they made together, *The Salamander* is a wry pleasure: a teasing tale of people and their social relations, at once subversive but never didactic. Exploring the fault line between rumour and reality in an alleged shooting, the film digresses wonderfully to follow the suspected assailant – a shopgirl (Bulle Ogier, excellent) – and the world she occupies.

The Middle of the World Le Milieu du Monde

Switzerland-France 1974/Dir Alain Tanner. With Olimpia Carlisi, Philippe Léotard, Juliet Berto.

117 mins.

SAT 16 APR 3.00 NFT2

MON 18 APR 8.40 NFT2

This second in the Berger/Tanner collaborative trilogy is the most narratively conventional of the

three. However, in its charting of an affair between a waitress and a married local politico hungry for more, there's an impressive synchronicity with the wintry absences of the landscape and the ultimately tragic struggle for independence. Of its decade in terms of mood, it's nevertheless a deeply empathetic and quietly optimistic work.

Jonah Who Will be 25 in the Year 2000 Jonas, Qui Aura 25 Ans en L'An 2000

Switzerland-France 1975/Dir Alain Tanner. With Jean-Luc Bideau, Rufus, Miou-Miou, Jacques Denis.

115 mins.

SAT 16 APR 6.00 NFT2

WED 20 APR 6.00 NFT2

One of the most important films of its decade and now being rediscovered in a new age of political engagement, *Jonah...* is perhaps the most humane radical feature yet made. Following the lives of eight characters all affected by the events and spirit of May 1968, it's an honest, often humorous and movingly committed exploration of diverse attempts to reconcile life and ideals.

Pig Earth + Parting Shots from Animals

SAT 16 APR 8.40 NFT3

MON 25 APR 6.10 NFT2*

Perhaps Berger's finest TV essay, *Pig Earth* (Omnibus; BBC 1979/Dir Mike Dibb; 50 mins) is both praise song and threnody to peasant life. Like the book, it's a collaboration with Jean Mohr, whose stills and super-8 footage

enthrall. Studiously anti-nostalgic, it closes with an invocation to the new peasantry: the freedom fighters in Algeria and Vietnam. Running alongside various essays written throughout Berger's career, *Parting Shots* (Omnibus; BBC 1980/Dir Mike Dibb; 50 mins) flips the camera and looks at humans – and their growing solitary confinement – from the perspective of animals.

Total 100 mins.

* Introduction by Mike Dibb.

About Time: Once Upon a Time + Crumbling Houses Visioni di case che crollano + 12 August 2002

SUN 17 APR 2.50 NFT2

A deliriously vagrant episode from this important series (C4 1985/Dir Mike Dibb; 54 mins), exercising to the fullest its imaginative right to roam, that illuminates and builds upon the insights on storytelling, art and time raised by Berger's most distinctive book, *And Our Faces, My Heart, Brief as Photos*. Plus Gianni Celati's lyrical essay on memory, history and the mutability of things (Italy 2003; 51 mins), taking as its subject the decline of communities in the Po river valley and the attendant dereliction of the region's farms and houses. Berger offers an on-location commentary that builds on his own lifelong concerns as a writer. In *12 August 2002* (Belgium 2002/Dir Milena Trivier; 9 mins), the demolition of a tower prompts thoughts on the moment we're living through.

Total 114 mins.

Another Way of Telling: Views of Photography +
I Send You This Cadmium Red
MON 18 APR 5.50 NFT2
SUN 24 APR 5.40 NFT2*

A fascinating collaboration with director John Christie and photographer Jean Mohr, this illuminating four part series (BBC 1989; 4x30 mins) of 'postcards' on all aspects of the photographic image and its relation to experience draws on Berger and Mohr's important book of the same name, which sought to create a new form of photographic narrative. The films take up the challenge and deliver a compelling weave of ideas and reflections. Plus a short (UK 2002/Dir John Christie; 8 mins) drawn from the stunning book and Radio 3 programme of the same name: a meditation on the implications of colour.
Total 128 mins.

*Introduction by John Christie.

John Berger in Conversation
TUE 19 APR 6.20 NFT1

In a rare on-stage interview appearance, the hugely influential writer will be in extended conversation with acclaimed novelist and critic Geoff Dyer, who has written widely about Berger's work, its reach and importance. Part of 'Here Is Where We Meet', a London-wide season celebrating Berger's work in all media (visit www.johnberger.org for more details).

Joint ticket available with *Play Me Something* (Tue 19 Apr only) £10.50, concs £8.25.

Play Me Something

UK 1989/Dir Timothy Neat. With JB, Lucia Lanzarini, Charlie Barron, Hamish Henderson, Tilda Swinton.
72 mins. J-Cert 15.
TUE 19 APR 8.20 NFT1*
SAT 23 APR 6.20 NFT2

This little seen but widely admired meditation on people, places, love, politics, culture and the whole damn thing sees Berger in compelling performance mode as a storyteller, diverting the handful of passengers awaiting the Glasgow plane from the Hebridean island of Barra. Shot in multiple formats to convey the textures of time and memory, it's a poignant and resolutely independent British film.

*Introduction by Timothy Neat.

Special ticket offer with John Berger in Conversation.

Caught Between Culture and Commerce? Independent Film and Television in the UK and Beyond Panel Discussion
TUE 26 APR 6.20 NFT2

With John Berger's innovative work in features and documentary television in mind, this wide-ranging panel will consider the health of independent filmmaking in this country. With format television dominating broadcast, and a dearth of funds for 'arthouse' cinema, can imaginative and committed new film-makers survive in today's accountant-run arenas? With documentary maker Mike Dibb, critic Chris Darke, writer Colin MacCabe, director Sally Potter (tbc) and others to be confirmed. Moderated by the co-editor of *Vertigo* magazine, Holly Aylett, this discussion will be preceded

by a screening of the John Berger/Mike Dibb and Chris Rawlence TV collaboration *About Time: Once Upon a Time* (54 mins; see p16), introduced by Dibb and Christopher Rawlence.

A Telling Eye: The Work of John Berger +
Germinal
WED 27 APR 8.20 NFT2
SAT 30 APR 6.20 NFT2*

This overview essay by Berger's long-standing filmic collaborator (BBC 1994/Dir Mike Dibb; 60 mins) helpfully traces the diverse strands of Berger's career, and includes tributes from Marina Warner and Geoff Dyer, plus an interview with the late Susan Sontag. *Germinal* (*The Nineteenth Century Novel and Its Legacy*; BBC 1983; 23 mins), a riveting programme made for the Open University, sees Berger revisiting Zola's 1872 social classic by descending a Derbyshire coalmine. Ever the scrupulous self-interrogator, he challenges the idea of documentary itself ('always an outsider's view'), before advocating actual experience as a mode of knowledge.
Total 83 mins.

*Introduction by Mike Dibb.

The Spectre of Hope +
John Berger in Conversation with Michael Ondaatje +
His Name Is Tyler
THU 28 APR 5.50 NFT2
FRI 29 APR 8.30 NFT2*

Two conversations here, formally extremely simple, but remarkably far-ranging and often moving documents of the complex

relationship between art and life. In the first (Arena; BBC 2001/Dir Paul Carlin; 60 mins), Berger talks with the great Brazilian photographer Sebastiao Salgado about his stunning humanitarian images. The second (USA 2003/ The Lannan Foundation; 40 mins) sees Berger and acclaimed novelist Michael Ondaatje reflect on the nature and mystery of writing. Plus a short from the Slot Art series (C4 2001/Dir Paul Carlin; 3 mins) in which Berger reads from his own work.
Total 103 mins.

*Introduction by Paul Carlin.

The Three Lives of Lucie Cabrol
FRI 29 APR 5.20 NFT2
SAT 30 APR 8.10 NFT2*

The first in a profound and ongoing series of performative collaborations between Berger and internationally renowned theatre director Simon McBurney of Complicité, this enormously successful adaptation of Berger's stories about peasant life in Europe played at Hammersmith's Riverside Studios. This previously unseen three-camera edited version of the stage performance (UK 1995/Dir Mike Dibb; 120 mins) faithfully conveys the impressive live experience. Plus a short *Late Show* (BBC 1995; 10 mins) item on the production.
Total c130 mins.

*Introduction by Simon McBurney and members of the cast.

National Film Theatre, South Bank, London, SE1. Box office: 020 7928 3232; www.bfi.org.uk/nft